OCEAN LINERS

This edition published in North America in 1999
by Chartwell Books, Inc.
a Division of Book Sales, Inc.
118 Northfield Avenue
Edison, NJ 08837
© Copyright Paris 1998

ISBN: 0-7858-1086-2
Printed in Spain

OCEAN LINERS

By
Olivier Le Goff

With technical assistance from
Claude Molteni de Villermont

English translation by Roger Jones

CHARTWELL
BOOKS, INC

CONTENTS

The Titanic

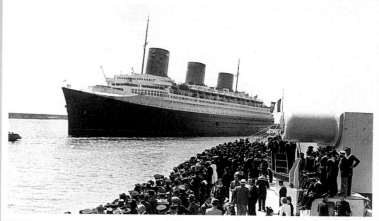

The Normandie

4

C O N T E N T S

The Grand Princess

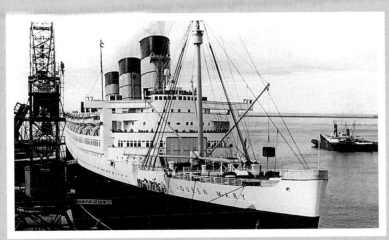

The Queen Mary

FROM THE SAILING SHIPS TO LINERS

On September 16, 1620,
a sailing ship set out from
Southampton for the
New World, then a British
possession. When the
occupants of the vessel
dropped anchor in this
new Promised Land, they
named their landing place
Plymouth, and this became
the center of their colony.
The United States, still
a young nation, needed
to create heroes for itself.
Its history celebrates the epic
of the Pilgrim Fathers,
a hundred or so Puritans,
who are forever associated
with the *Mayflower,* the
ship on which they made
the crossing in sixty six days.
After these pioneers,
the ocean was to witness
a succession of colonists,
immigrants, travellers
and tourists. These were the
passengers who travelled
on the liners, the fascinating
evolution of which is closely
associated with the social
upheavals of the last
500 years.
But let us return to the
beginning of the 19th century
to pay homage to the many
men and great technical
advances that enabled the
ocean liner industry to thrive
over the next century.

6

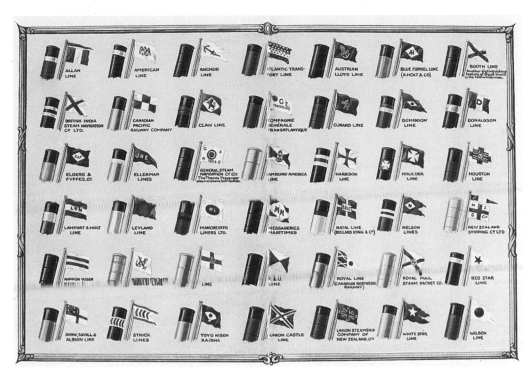

Nearly a century separates the Savannah (facing page), the first ship to use steam power, from the shipping companies of the great age of liners, whose colors can be seen on the left.

Robert Fulton

Steam

After the *Mayflower,* sailing ships underwent many technological advances in terms of rigging and dimensions, but the duration of a voyage remained completely dependent on the wind, and varied considerably according to whether one was sailing eastwards or westwards.

The greatest innovation was to come with steam, although it is difficult to know who first discovered the principle of its use. The notion of using the motive force of water vapour is ancient, going back to the first century AD. It was at this time that Hero of Alexandria built the first steam engine. The apparatus, called an *eolipile,* remains a curiosity with no practical application.

It was not until the 17th century that the idea resurfaced. In 1687, Denis Papin lighted upon a theory to describe a machine to pump water. His principle relied on the movement of a piston which was activated by steam. In 1698, Thomas Savery, an Englishman, registered a patent for a suction pump. This single cylinder apparatus represented the first practical application of steam, working by steam and atmospheric pressure. Thomas Newcomen returned to this principle in 1705.

The father of steam, who was involved in the development of the Industrial Revolution, was James Watt. He invented the condenser, as well as the flywheel, to maintain a constant pressure in the boilers of the first steam engines.

The application of steam to sailing ships, however evolved more slowly. The Englishman Jonathan Hulls registered the patents for the first tug to be driven by paddle wheels in 1736. In 1783, Joffroy d'Abbans, a French marquis, managed to run his pyroscaphe, a side paddler. William Symington of Scotland gave a haulage demonstration with his tug, the *Charlotte Dundas,* and in 1787, the American James Rumsey made the first pump jet motor, which drew in water at the prow and released it from the poop.

In 1803, the American Robert Fulton launched a steam barge on the Seine—a "water chariot moved by fire." Because of the lack of interest the demonstration aroused, however, this pioneer—who had already planned the ancestor of the submarine in 1798—left for the United States, disappointed with France, whose Revolution he had greatly admired.

The *Savannah*

The first successful application of steam to a ship occurred on May 24, 1819, when the *Savannah* set out from the town of the same name in Georgia. This 320 ton ship, had classic rigging plus an auxiliary motor, collapsible paddle wheels, and an adjustable funnel that was designed to prevent the sails from catching fire. She managed to reach Liverpool in 27 days, 18 hours, carrying only 75 tons of coal and 90 cubic meters of wood on board as back-up. The steam engine it-

The Sirius.

self only ran for 72 hours in total during the crossing.

Equipped and commanded by Moses Rogers, the *Savannah* used sailpower for most of the crossing, except for the rare periods when the sea was too calm. As the ship approached the Irish port of Kinsale under steam, however the coastguards became frightened by the smoke and believed the approaching ship to be on fire.

Although a large crowd collected to welcome the *Savannah* into the port at Liverpool, the ship was viewed as only a mere experiment by certain professionals. There was no readiness to admit that steam could, in fact, play a major role in an Atlantic crossing, even though small steam vessels were already being used for short crossings. However, Rogers decided to take advantage of the curiosity his ship excited and tried to sell it. Despite a tour of the Nordic countries, he did not find any buyer in Europe. The following year, an American buyer stripped the *Savannah* of her engines and used her a sailing boat. She sank in 1821.

And so the idea of steam navigation entered the realms of the spirits and the *Savannah* became a mythical ship for the Americans.

The *Royal William*

The *Royal William* marked the next stage of steam navigation. This Canadian ship was built in 1831 to provide a regular service between Quebec and Nova Scotia. Disappointed with the revenues earned by the boat, however, its new owner decided to sell it in England in 1833. She left Quebec on August 4 with seven passengers, and then left Pictou, Nova Scotia on August 18, after taking on a load of coal. She reached the Thames estuary on September 9, and London three days later. The ship had run on steam for three quarters of its Atlantic crossing; the sails had only been used during the long periods in which the engines had to be stopped so the insides of the boilers could be scrubbed of the accumulated salt.

The First Competition: the *Sirius* versus the *Great Western*

The year 1838 marked the beginning of competition on the Atlantic route. The ship that accomplished the first crossing entirely by steam was the *Sirius,* a small vessel of around 700 tons and 52 meters in length. Leaving Liverpool on April 3 and Cork, Ireland on April 4 with 94 passengers and 31 crew, she reached New York on April 22. Right to the end, Captain Rogers refused to use her sails; having used the 453 tons of coal in the bunkers plus 53 barrels of resin, he did not hesitate to burn the furniture and safety rigging in order to finish the voyage under steam.

The *Sirius'* success was in great part due to the stubbornness of her captain, who paid no regard to either the discontent of the passengers, who were bothered by the smell and the rolling, or to the beginnings of a mutiny, which he ended quickly by threatening the crew with a pistol. This ship was also equipped with a steam condensation device which provided fresh water, so there was no need to resort to laborious operations to scrub off the salt.

At the same time the Great Western Steamship Company was waiting to put into service a new ship, launched in 1837, and designed by Isambard Brunel, a British engineer of French ancestry. This was a considerably larger vessel than the *Sirius;* weighing 1,320 tons and stretching 64.6 meters (236 feet) in length, it was equipped with four masts and had a two-cylinder steam engine to drive the paddle wheels. The *Great Western,* though faster than her rival, set off on March 31, 1838, but had to turn back following a fire. She was not able to resume her maiden voyage until April 8. Although she did not gain a place in history as the first liner to cross the Atlantic under steam, she still took the Blue Riband with a speed of eight knots.

Mail Steamers

The establishment of a regular service across the Atlantic with these two steam ships demonstrated the superiority of steam over sail. However, for a long time these ships retained auxiliary rigging; it was only with the approach of the First World War that most of the shipping fleet was propelled mechanically, with the masts serving only to accommodate the crow's nest and flags.

In any case, this newly acquired advantage of speed and punctuality aroused interest from postal services everywhere. This regularity would eventually be underwritten with government subsidies, and these ships would play an important role in the development of powerful companies.

Peninsular and Oriental (P & O) was formed after an exclusive contract was granted to the Penninsular Steam Navigation Company for the transportation of British mail to Portugal and Spain.

The company, which is still in existence, is best known today for its fleet of liners, ferries and container ships.

In a similar manner, Samuel Cunard, who had only owned a fleet of sailing ships, gained the concession for a postal service between Great Britain and the United States in

ISAMBARD KINGDOM BRUNEL

Brunel, one of the most genial inventors of all time, was born in 1806. His father, a Frenchman who emigrated to England after the Revolution, was also an engineer. Isambard started his career on land, which was witnessing the development of the railways and other major projects at the time. He is credited with completing a tunnel under the Thames (which his father had started), as well as the construction of 130 bridges and 25 railway lines. It was his career in railways that enabled Brunel to become a great naval architect. During this particular stage of the industrial revolution, sea routes were becoming a natural extension of the rail stations that served the ports. His first naval design, the *Great Western*, was owned by an offshoot of the Great Western Railways. Nicknamed "the little giant", Brunel quickly made people forget his height (5 feet, 4 inches) with his undeniable geniality and a top hat that he never seemed to be without. The imagination of this visionary appeared to have no limits, even when the funds of the company's shareholders did. Although the three ships he designed continue to stand out in the history of steam shipping, they were also the cause of heavy financial losses. Brunel was clearly too advanced for his time.

9

The Great Western.

SAMUEL CUNARD

Born in Halifax, Nova Scotia, Samuel Cunard belonged to a family of Quakers who had been driven out of England in the 17th century. With his father, who was a master ship's carpenter by origin, Cunard purchased his first boat for the purpose of coastal navigation between Canada and the United States. The development of his fleet led him to establish Samuel Cunard & Co in 1820. But the businessman in Cunard did not stop there. Puting his faith in the steam industry, he placed orders for four ships (the *Britannia, Arcadia, Caledonia* and *Columbia*) with Napier, a British naval engineer. Cunard financed the project by founding the Cunard Line and signed a contract with the British Admiralty for the transportation the mail. This was the start of an amazing expansion of a company which placed punctuality and safety before speed. Since its establishment, the Cunard company has not suffered a single death on board due to accidents in peacetime.

Samuel Cunard, founder of the first transatlantic steamer company.

1839. He pulled off the deal after raising enough capital to create the British & North American Steam Packet Company, more commonly known as the Cunard Line. The sailing ship owner had now become the manager of a steamer company.

Meanwhile, France needed to make up for lost time. In 1851, the Compagnie de Messageries Maritimes began to run a postal service along the Mediterranean and then to

The Britannia.

The name of the Pereire brothers is bound up with the expansion created by the Industrial Revolution and the prosperity enjoyed by the Second Empire. They played a particularly important role in the development of railroads and were responsible for the creation of the town of Arachon, thanks to the railroad infrastructure they gave to the site. They were the people to whom Napoleon III had turned to set up a transatlantic postal service between France and the United States. (He wanted to make up for the failure of a company founded in 1847 by Herout and Handel from Le Havre.) Through the Société Generale de Crédit Mobilier they managed, the two banker brothers would take a 50% holding in the Compagnie Generale Maritime which was established in 1855; the rest of the capital was subscribed to by private shareholders. The company, renamed the Compagnie Generale Atlantique in 1861, gained the concessions for the North American and Central American routes and subsidies, provided they placed orders for half of the ships in France. It is as a result of this clause that the Penhoät Shipyard near Saint Nazaire was created. The Pereire brothers, dissatisfied with the estimates from French yards compared to those of foreign competitors, established their own yard which built only the hulls for ships.

11

Latin America. In 1861, France obtained the concession between Suez, whose canal had recently opened, and the Far East, which was a new area of interest for the French. It was not until 1860, under the reign of Napoleon III, that the Pereire brothers created the Compagnie Generale Maritime, after obtaining from the imperial government the postal service concession between France and the American continent.

The Metal Hull

The launch of ever larger ships is explained by a technical problem due to displacement—the weight of water displaced. The greater the displacement, the better the stability, and with the same power it is possible to attain greater speeds with lower fuel consumption. However, building larger ships of wood led to problems of structural fragility, as the hull was subjected to greater stresses in high seas.

In view of the regularity of the crossings and the increasing numbers of passengers, it made sense to increase the tonnage for the benefit not of the hull, which was considered a dead weight, but of the propulsion and fittings. The solution here was to build a metal hull. The *Aaron Manly* was the first ship to be built with an iron hull, but it was only used on a very short route between Great Britain and France. A short distance

such as this did not enable the iron hull to demonstrate its superiority in terms of large tonnages, and it was not until 1845 that the iron hull appeared on a transatlantic liner.

In the early 1880s, iron would give way to steel. The hull, which represented half the total tonnage when a ship was built of wood, only accounted for one third when steel was used. As well, metal offered two new advantages with regard to safety: in allowing interior partitioning it increased the rigidity of the structure, and in enabling double bottomed hulls to be constructed it limited the risk of sinking in a collision.

The Great Britain.

The *Great Britain*

Built by Isambard Kingdom Brunel, the *Great Britain* was the first transatlantic ship to have a double iron hull. This innovation gave rise to strong misgivings at her departure, however, and this is why for her inaugural crossing in 1845 she only took sixty passengers (although designed for six times as many.)

With her six masts, this liner was the first to be driven by a propeller. When she originally entered service, she was the largest ship in the world, stretching 98.1 meters (289 feet) in lenght and weighing 3,618 tons. Yet despite her impressive qualifications, she did not make money for her owners and was sold after being grounded off the Irish coast for over six months, following technical problems after her launch.

Her subsequent career typifies the kinds of transformations liners undergo after a period of inactivity. The *Great Britain* was later put on the Australia route, and then—with her engine removed, on coal transportation duties—to California. From 1886 to 1937, she served as a floating warehouse in the Falkland Islands. Then, after a long period of neglect, she was towed to Bristol, England, the city where she had been built and where her original owner was based. Today, fully restored, she is still anchored in the port of Bristol. Together with the *Queen Mary,* the *Great Britain* is one of the rare examples of a liner that, having escaped shipwreck and demolition, continues a sedentary existence.

The contribution of the Collins Line

Despite its brief existence, the Collins Line was the only American company to make its mark on the history of liners in the 19th century.

The Dramatic Line had been created by Edward Knight Collins in the 1830s. He converted his fleet, originally consisting of sailing ships, to steam after obtaining an American mail concession between New York and Liverpool.

Unlike Samuel Cunard, who had stressed reliability and safety without ostentation, Collins deliberately went in for magnificence. It was he who came up with the idea for the luxury style on liners, both in the fittings as well as the cuisine, that would be found on the floating palaces of the twentieth century. Another innovation of his was the installation of the first cold store—for preserving food on the ships—in 1848 (refrigeration did not become common until the 1880s). It is difficult to imagine the conditions that prevailed on an Atlantic crossing prior to that date, with cattle below deck, which were slaughtered as needed during the course of the voyage, as well as plenty of chickens and cows to provide eggs and milk.

When placing orders for his new steamers, Collins also placed much emphasis on speed, which enabled him to gain the Blue Riband twice, in 1848 with the *Atlantic* and in 1851 with the *Pacific*.

Thanks to their speed and the quality of service provided, the Collins Line ships enjoyed a great deal of commercial success. Unfortunately, this venture was not profitable and the company soon began to lose money. Two events in particular precipitated its demise. In September, 1854, the *Arctic*

13

The Great-Britain wrecked on the Irish coast.

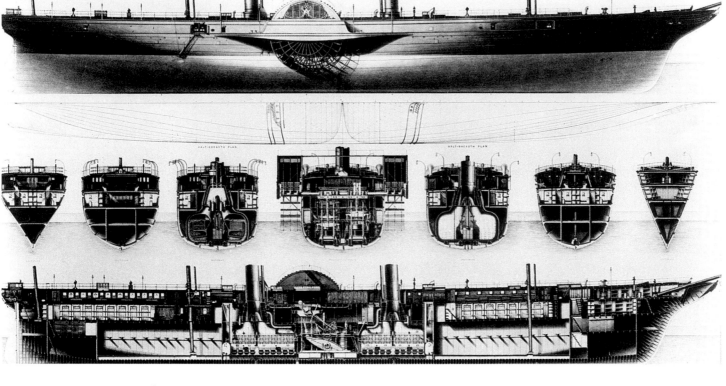

BRITISH & NORTH AMERICAN ROYAL MAIL STEAM SHIP "PERSIA" CONSTRUCTED BY MESSRS R. NAPIER & SONS, GLASGOW.

THE PROPELLER

The propeller was an important technical improvement over paddle wheels, which were very heavy, fragile and sensitive to rough seas, and better suited for river navigation. The idea that was originally taken from Archimedes' worm screw underwent many modifications before the adoption of the ideal number of blades —four—to give the optimum performance. In 1868, a liner was equipped with two propellers for the first time. This was Transat's *Washington,* which was originally equipped with paddle wheels which were removed when the propellers were fitted. These propellers gave the ship greater autonomy even if one of them failed, and this quickened the demise of auxiliary sails at the end of the 19th century. Transat's *Touraine,* launched in 1891, was the last liner to be equipped in this way.

was sunk off of Newfoundland after being struck by the *Vesta,* a small French steamer with one tenth of her tonnage. Between 280 and 360 voyagers perished, including Collins' wife and two children and five members of his partner's family.

In June, 1856, the *Pacific,* bound from Liverpool to New York, was lost in her entirety, taking with her 45 passengers and 141 crew members.

These two catastrophes played a big part in prompting the introduction of the metal hull (the four ships Collins ordered were of traditional design with paddle wheels and wooden hulls). By contrast, the small *Vesta,* which had an iron hull, managed to extricate herself and reach a Canadian port. As for the *Pacific,* her hull was recovered from the Irish Sea in 1986, 130 years after she sank. Until then, it was assumed that she had collided with an iceberg. A similar event occurred at exactly the same time without loss of life, involving the Cunard Line's *Persia,* which had an iron hull and, in addition, took the Blue Riband in 1856.

The *Great Eastern*

The design of this giant boat, the last that was attributable to Brunel, was also the most prestigious. From its launch in 1860, the *Great Eastern* remained the largest ship in the world until the *Celtic,* belonging to the White Star Line, came into service in 1901. Stretching 210 meters (698 feet) in length, her dimensions exceeded those of the *Kaiser Wilhelm der Grosse* and the *Deutschland,* both of which were considered monsters when they were launched at the turn of the century.

The *Great Eastern* was one of those liners whose entire career was bedevilled with bad luck, yet her history was extraordinary. Brunel, her genial and megalomaniacal inventor, wanted to build an immense ship that was capable of carrying enough coal to reach Australia, then a very important destination for emigrants. With her five funnels, six masts, a propeller and two paddle wheels, this ship made such an impression on Jules Verne that he made her the heroine of his novel, *A Floating City.*

The *Great Eastern's* first victim was her inventor, who went bankrupt before the ship's launch on the Thames on January 30, 1858. On that day, a large crowd had gathered to watch the event. The ship's manoeuvres had already cost the lives of two workmen, and

Brunel realized that when the ship entered the river, it would submerge the crowds on the lower shores of the bank. He managed to stop the launch, but the liner remained stuck for three months before she finally reached the water. This loss of earnings was sufficient to bankrupt her owners.

A year went by before she found a new owner, and the ship left the Thames for Liverpool on September 9, 1859, (it was not until the beginning of the twentieth century that Southampton, with a deeper basin and less dependent on the tides, became the principal port for travelers from Great Britain). During this voyage, which was quite modest compared with the crossings planned, an explosion in a boiler caused the deaths of five people on board, and a sixth on land. Subsequently, Brunel died upon hearing the news, having suffered a stroke the month

Facing page:
Transverse and longitudinal sections of the Persia, designed in 1860. Note the large area occupied by the engines of this ship.
Below:
The Great Eastern.

15

THE *GREAT EASTERN* AS SEEN BY JULES VERNE

"This steam ship is a masterpiece of naval construction. It is more than a vessel, it is a floating city, part of a county detached from English soil, which after crossing the sea will become attached to American soil (...)

"Three or four coalers drawn up alongside her fill her bunkers, open above the waterline with their cargo of coal. Next to the *Great Eastern*, these three-masters seem like small boats. Their funnels do not reach the first row of portholes in her hull. Their topsails do not reach her bulwarks (...)

"... I skirted these superstructures which stretched out on the stern of the ship. Between them and the ship's rail on each side were two wide roads, or rather boulevards, jammed with a dense crowd. I arrived at the center of the vessel between the barrels connected by a double system of gangways. There

the space opened up which would contain the equipment of the paddle wheel engine. I then saw this admirable locomotion engine. Fifty workmen were spread over the metallic tracery of the cast-iron frame, some attached to long pistons set at different angles, others hanging from connecting rods, adjusting the crank, using enormous spanners to bolt the shaft bearings. This metal trunk, which came down slowly through the hatch, was a new shaft which would transmit the movement of the rods to the wheels. A continuous noise came out of this abyss, made up of shrill and discordant sounds. (...)

"After twenty crossings between England and America, one of which was clouded by very grave events, the operation of the *Great Eastern* was abandoned for a time, This immense ship intended for the transportation of passengers no longer seemed good for anything and looked

as if she would be sent for scrap by its mistrustful overseas passengers. When the first attempts to lay a telegraph cable under the Atlantic failed—oartly due to the lack of ships to transport it—the engineers thought of the *Great Eastern*. She alone could carry on board the 3,400 kilometres (2,125 miles) of metal cable weighing 4,500 tons. She alone, thanks to her complete indifference to the sea, could roll out and submerge this immense cable. But in order to stow the cable in the sides of the ship, special adjustments had to be made. Two of the six boilers were taken out, as was one of the three funnels belonging to the propeller's engine. In their place vast containers were placed to hold the cable in which a sheet of water protected from changes in the air. The wire passed through these floating lakes without making contact with atmospheric layers. The laying of the cable was carried out successfully ..."

Contrary to his custom, Jules Verne did not use his imagination in A Floating City. *Telling only the story he had experienced, he left all the creativity to its designer, Isambard Kingdom Brunel.*

before. But the carnage did not stop there. In January, 1860, eleven crew members drowned when a launch taking them to terra firma capsized.

The *Great Eastern* had not even made her first crossing when her new owner went bankrupt. A new company soon threw itself into the adventure but limited its ambitions to the transatlantic run. On June 17, 1860, the liner finally left for New York with a full crew and only 35 ticketed passengers, whereas Brunel had made provision for five thousand.

Although arousing a great deal of curiosity, the *Great Eastern,* which suffered an incurable roll, never attracted a large enough clientele to make her financially viable. To this public disaffection was added ill luck. In 1861, the ship fell victim to a storm, which entailed a long period in dock, and in 1862 she foundered on a reef. This latter incident is of interest in that it demonstrates theadvantages of a double hull, which was made possible by the use of iron. Eventually, the discouraged owner sold her at an auction. She was then used to lay the first transatlantic telegraph cable, which, after one failure, was completed in 1866. In 1867, France chartered her to bring American visitors to the World Exhibition in Paris. This was her final two-way crossing, in which Jules Verne participated. The size of the commercial catastrophe surrounding this enterprise was such that the ship never again took to the seas.

It was eventually in port at the mouth of the River Mersey that the *Great Eastern* proved to be most profitable. Her hull, which advertised a large Liverpool store, was used as a floating fairground. In 1887, it was destined for demolition, which took place the following year. But her history did not finish there. As she was being dismantled, the remains of two workmen were found trapped in the double hull. At Scott Russell's, the original builders of the *Great Eastern,* the unexplained disappearance of two members of staff was finally solved.

17

Germany: Birth of a Naval Nation

In Germany, the 1850s saw the establishment of two companies that would play an important role in the history of the liner: the Hamburg-Amerikanische Paketfahrt Aktien Gesellschaft (HAPAG or Hamburg Amerika Line) in 1847 and Norddeutscher Lloyd (NDL or North German Lloyd) in 1857. Their headquarters were in Hamburg and Bremen respectively, two of the great North Sea ports. Their prosperity was originally due to the flow of emigrants to America, first the Germans and Scandinavians, then Eastern Europeans.

The accession of Kaiser Wilhelm II considerably accelerated the German's breakthough on to the seas. On June 15, 1888, the day of his accession, he wrote to his brother, a grand admiral, "I shall not rest until I have raised the navy to the level of the army." This ambition applied equally to the merchant fleet, thanks in particular to Albert Ballin, who became the emperor's adviser. At Dantzig in 1898, Wilhelm II reaffirmed his conviction declaring, "Our future is on the water."

It was this alliance between political and economic power that would bring the Germans to rival the British in luxury, size and speed, and enable them to win the Blue Riband.

Above: HAPAG poster.

18

Coal's grandeur
and servitude

As the original fuel used in liners to which they owe their development, coal occupied a very important role in the economy of the 19th century. To a great extent it explains the lead taken by the British, who had ample deposits, most notably in Wales.

If the translatlantic liners have enjoyed the most legendary status of all, it is because an ocean crossing has no stopping-off points. This meant that a ship would carry enough coal to be autonomous, so the use of sails disappeared gradually. The amount of coal required became greater and greater.

Loading a ship with coal was done either by using dockside labour or directly from a coaling ship. In both cases, the operation produced polluting coal dust and the ships required a thorough clean up afterwards. This explains why the hulls were painted black—liners as well as cargo ships. Once loaded with coke, the ships were ready for the crossing, and the coal trimmers got ready to experience hell. The stoking roads were spaces that supplied all the boilers, where the working conditions were very trying. The temperature could reach 40° to 50°C on the North Atlantic and 70°C in tropical seas. Unlike wooden hulls, metal hulls, offered poor insulation. The engineers were obliged to be at their workplace regardless of weather conditions and the state of the sea, in order to maintain the expected speed.

Speed was not a matter that was taken lightly. With increasing competition between companies, it became necessary to take on more and more coal. In fact, consumption did not increase in a linear fashion; it was exponential. For example, in order to double the ship's speed it was not sufficient to merely double the amount of coal. The problem arose most notably around the fateful threshold of 20 knots, which was achieved at the end of the 1880s. To sustain such a speed, eight times as the normal amount of coal was needed.

As coal consumption increased to greater proportions, ships' bunders had to be enlarged. At the same time, the passenger areas had to become larger, since the increase in speed attracted a new kind of clientele.

At the beginning of the twentieth century, advertisements for the new liners focused particular attention to the passengers' needs. One artist depicted the *Mauretania* behind 24 trains carrying the coal required for a single transatlantic crossing—6,600 tons of fuel, admittedly for a ship that kept the Blue Riband for 20 years.

One company director estimated that above a certain speed, coal could cost more than caviar. To gain an extra knot cost an exorbitant amount, which could only be recovered by appealing for state support. These ships were so important as symbols of power and prestige that the governments of every country concerned subsidised their national shipping companies, both to pay for the regular transportation of mail and to permit the construction of ships that could be modified for military use in times of war.

The turbine

The turbine, which established the superiority of the rotary movement over the alternating movement, overcame the defects of the earlier engines that had limited scope for increasing performance, were very cumbersome and caused vibrations.

Invented by the British engineer Charles Parsons, who perfected it in 1884, the turbine came through her trials in a dazzling fashion at the Naval Review at Spithead in 1897. Parsons' yacht, the *Turbinia*, the first ship to be so equipped, proved to be so fast she outperformed all the other ships and,

most impressively, the torpedoes that tried to intercept her. Cunard then installed turbines in the *Lusitania* and the *Mauretania*, and this technology was quickly adopted Parson's death was worthy of the great engineer he was. He passed away in Jamaica on board the *Duchess of Richmond*, belonging to the Canadian Pacific Line, a liner with reduction turbines.

*

These few pages have focused on the outstanding events which punctuated the history of liners in the 19th century. The performances of the ships which gained the Blue Riband eloquently demonstrate the technical progress made. The *Savannah* crossed the Atlantic in just over 27 days in 1819; the *Britannia* in 10 days from Halifax, Nova Scotia to Liverpool in 1840; the *Persia* in nine days in 1856; and in 1888, the *City of Paris* broke through the six day threshold.

The remainder of the story is about the finest liners ever built, those of the 20th century. Has travel now become an anti-social act, as Paul Morand has claimed? Probably not, if we consider the lively days so many people have spent on these floating palaces.

Note

In the following pages the reader will find for each liner a technical specification indicating her main characteristics: length, width, tonnage, speed, passenger capacity and crew (sailors and stewards).

This data refers to the liner as she entered service as a merchant ship. Over the course of a ship's career, however, these characteristics are often subject to modification.

19

Cunard advertisement showing sea routes as a naturel extension of the railroad.

THE PRECURSORS

At the beginning of the twentieth century, Britain was extremely shaken by the loss of her merchant shipping supremacy to Germany, whose improved performance was given impetus by the close co-operation between Kaiser Wilhelm and Alfred Ballin, president of the Hamburg-Amerika Line. This complete change of circumstances affected the transportation of emigrants, who provided the financial cushion to enable the shipping company to balance its books, as much as the revenue from the transportation of wealthy clients provided, who were attracted by the speed and magnificence of the German vessels. With the involvement of their shipping companies, the two countries embarked on a relentless competition for speed and customer service. In material resources, Germany and Great Britain occupied the greater part of the field, leaving France and the United States far behind, with fewer vessels performing less successfully on the prestigeous North Atlantic route. This race can be seen as a foreshadowing of the major conflict, which from 1914 onwards would be played out with a new weapon: the submarine.

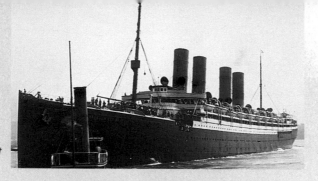

The funnel of the tug offers an idea of the proportions of the first "ocean greyhound".

THE RESULT OF POLITICAL WILLPOWER

From his accession to the imperial throne in 1888, King Wilhelm II could not rest until he had made the German navy the most powerful in the world, in both the military and commercial spheres. In 1889, HAPAG delivered the first liner built by a German shipyard. This was the *Augusta Victoria*, built at the Vulkan Yard in Stettin and named in honor of the Empress. The ship was 141 meters long and 17 meters wide. However, during the same year on a visit to the British naval review at Spithead, Wilhelm II was greatly impressed by the new *Teutonic* as he stood on its bridge. This liner measured 582 feet (177 meters) in total. The Kaiser then decided to enter the race for size. The first two results of this ambition were the *Kaiser Wilhelm der Grosse* and, three years later, the *Deutschland.*

HONORING AN EMPEROR

The name *Kaiser Wilhelm der Grosse* was given in homage to Wilhelm I. After becoming King of Prussia in 1861, he was the first representative of the Second Reich after his coronation on January 18, 1871, at Versailles in the Gallery of Mirrors. Upon his death in 1888, his son succeeded him as Frederick III, but the new sovereign suffered from throat cancer and only reigned for 90 days before dying at the age of 57. The 29 year-old Wilhelm II then acceeded the throne and remained there until 1918, at the end of a world war characterized by a naval confrontation with the United Kingdom. The conflict broke out just thirteen years after the death of his maternal grandmother, Queen Victoria.

A TIME OF CALMS AND STORMS

On June 30, 1900, the liner was moored in New York when a huge fire broke out on the quay allocated to NDL; the ship was rescued from the flames in the nick of time. On November 21, In 1906, the *Kaiser Wilhelm der Grosse* was struck in foggy conditions by the *Orinoco* of the Royal Mail Lines. The British steamship which had a clipper stem was relatively unscathed but the German liner recorded five deaths and considerable damage.

Changing roles

Length: 199.4 meters
(655 feet)
Width: 20 meters
(62 feet)
Tonnage: 14,349 tons
Speed: 23 knots
Passengers: 1,550
Crew: 488 men

At the end of the 19th century, Germany held first place ahead of Britain in terms of the number of passengers on the Atlantic route. In 1897, Norddeutscher Lloyd delivered a new ship named *Kaiser Wilhelm der Grosse* in honor of Wilhelm I. Put on the North Atlantic route and calling at Cherbourg on alternate sailings on the outward and return trips, this prestigeous liner had a characteristic shape; it was the first time that a liner with four funnels had been put into service. Those on the *Kaiser Wilhelm* were grouped in pairs. This ship was also one of the first to be permanently equipped with a wireless telegraph in February, 1900, two years after the *Saint Paul.*

By 1897, after the delivery of the *Campania* and the *Lucania* in 1893, Cunard owned the fastest liners. The entry into service of the *Kaiser Wilhelm* on September 19, 1897, from Bremerhaven came as a thunderbolt in a sky dominated by the Union Jack. She was not only the biggest liner in the world, with a length exceeding in ex-

cess of 199.5 meters, but she also captured the Blue Riband from Cunard on her return crossing in November of that year.

In German, the achievement brought about a surge of patriotic enthusiasme and the publicity surrounding the event attracted an additional clientele. In Great Britain there was consternation as the end of British pre-eminence was confirmed with each record. This was the first German liner to impress the world with its speed, and it marked the emergence of a new naval power.

The grandiose Baroque decor of the *Kaiser Wilhelm* was created by Johannes Poppe. This was the first time a shipping company had entrusted the interior quarters of a ship to the tastes of one designer.

Built at the Vulkan Shipyard in Stettin, the *Kaiser Wilhelm der Grosse* was designed to carry 1,550 passengers (400 in first classe, 350 in second class and 800 in third class), with a crew of 500 (of whom more than 200 were engineers).

In 1903, she regained the Blue Riband from the *Deutschland,* owned by HAPAG, which had

captured it in 1900. Because of her speed and luxurious interior, the *Kaiser Wilhelm* remained the pride of the German merchant fleet until 1913, the year in which she was refitted to transport emigrants in third class.

The *Kaiser Wilhelm's* contribution to the First World War was somewhat ephemeral. Converted into an auxiliary cruiser at the beginning of August, 1914, she took part successfully in operations in the North Atlantic, although her heavy coal consumption was a handicap. But on August 26, 1916, she was ambushed at the mouth of the Rio D'Oro by the British cruiser, *Highflyer.* Following a series of skirmishes, the latter inflicted such damage on her that the German crew evacuated and scuttled the ship by blowing it up.

23

Officer of the Watch on the bridge of the Deutschland.

A SPEED CHAMPION

The *Deutschland* immediately made her presence felt as far as speed was concerned, gaining the Blue Riband from the *Kaiser Wilhelm der Grosse* on her maiden voyage. Thanks to her two propellers, driven by a quadruple expansion engine, she accomplished the crossing in 5 days, 15 hours and 46 minutes (at an average speed of 23.5 knots). In 1906, she undertook a race with *La Provence* of the Compagnie Generale Transatlantique (CGT), which came into service on the North Atlantic route in the same year. American millionaires placed bets on the outcome of the race, Rockefeller on the *Deutschland* and Vanderbilt's son on *La Provence.* It was *La Provence* that won the race by four hours, though the *Deutschland* did manage to attain the same speed which secured the Blue Riband for her competitor.

REGATTAS AND THE AMBASSADOR

Organized from the end of June to the beginning of July, the Kiel Regatta was a great event in the German social calendar that was attended by the Kaiser and his court. On this occasion, the *Victoria Luise* was used as a floating hotel. After the 1914 regatta, it was on this ship that the Austrian Ambassador heard news of the assassination of the heir to the throne, the Archduke Franz Ferdinand, and his wife at Sarajevo on June 28. The news completely disrupted the event and the British contingent withdrew from the competition. Five weeks later, the principal European belligerents declared war.

A History of Disillusionment

Length: 208.5 meters (684 feet)
Width: 20.4 meters (67 feet)
Tonnage: 16,502
Speed: 23.5 knots
Passengers: 2,100
Crew: 536 men

Just like the *Kaiser Wilhelm der Grosse*, the *Deutschland* was built by the Vulkan Shipyards at Stettin, but this time it was for the HAPAG company. With these two ships, Germany overtook Great Britain in regard to the size of the liners deployed on the transatlantic route. Compared with her Norddeutscher Lloyd rival, the *Deutschland* was 9 meters (30 feet) longer and of comparable width; the four funnels on this liner were grouped in pairs.

Originally, she was fitted to accommodate 2,100 passengers (450 in first class, 300 in second, 300 in third class and 1,050 emigrants).

When she came into service on the Hamburg - New York route *via* Plymouth on July 4, 1900, the *Deutschland* was the largest liner in Germany's commercial fleet. But to summarize the life of this elaborately decorated monster, we can simply say she embodied all the deceptions represented by successive modifications and its three changes of name.

It was quickly noticed that technically, the ship was not up to scratch. She was subject to strong vibrations which meant, to ensure the comfort of passengers, she could not operate at maximum speed. Top speed was only achieved at the cost of an excessive use of fuel.

From one name to another

In such conditions, the *Deutschland's* career lasted only a decade. In 1910, she underwent a year-long overhaul that tackled the ship's structural problems; the propulsion system was replaced by engines that ran at lower speeds; the passenger area was also revamped and the number of places reduced by three quarters, creating a single first-class ship.

With these changes, the ship no longer had the proper features for the transatlantic route. Moreover, she no longer deserved to fly high her country's flag by taking its name. So she started a second career as a luxury cruiser, equipped with launches of mahogany, after being renamed *Victoria Luise* in honor of one of Kaiser Wilhelm II's daughters. With the war came further humiliations. Although armed as an auxiliary cruiser, she was not used by the German Admiralty, who rated her performance poor. Finally, when

the Treaty of Versailles was signed in 1919 and war reparations were negotiated, she was accorded the ultimate snub: the Allies refused to take her because of her poor condition. Of all the great German liners, this is the only one that did not change its nationality.

The *Deutschland* was available for service, but she was worn out, and, more importantly, bore a regal name which was now out of place. She was taken out of service once more for a wide-ranging refit that amputated two of her funnels. In October, 1921, she returned to service under the name of *Hansa*, providing transatlantic crossings from Hamburg to the United States and then Canada for a clientele of emigrants. But this new career was of short duration, and she was laid up for good in 1924.

25

EMPRESS OF BRITAIN

The Pride of the Canadian Lines

**EMPRESS OF BRITAIN
EMPRESS OF IRELAND**

Length: 173.8 meters
(570 feet)
Width: 19.8 meters
(65 feet)
Tonnage: 14,190 tons
Passengers:
1,500 - 1,600
Crew: 400 men

The Canadian Pacific Lines was a British offshoot of the Canadian railroad and represented a natural extension to other continents. In 1881, the Canadian Pacific Railway Company was founded, which created Canadian Pacific Navigation two years later. Initially, the company's maritime activities were concentrated on Lake Superior and served by ships on lease. The year 1891 saw the start of its great transPacific service departing from Vancouver.

In 1906, the Canadian Pacific Line took delivery of two liners, which were to be the flagships of its fleet: the *Empress of Britain* and the *Empress of Ireland*. Built in Glasgow, these twin ships were the last transatlantic liners to have quadruple expansion engines prior to the advent of turbines. They were designed for normal categories of passengers, since they could accommodate 310 people in first class, 500 in second class, 500 in third class and 270 emigrants. The accommodations were less luxurious than that of the liners leaving New York, but they were still of a very good standard.

Equipped with two funnels and two propellers, these ships were put on the transatlantic route and completed their inaugural crossings in May and June, 1906.

The *Empress of Ireland's* career ended tragically in the spring of 1914, in a shipwreck that cost the lives of more than a thousand people.

The *Empress of Britain* served the route until she was reconfigured as an auxiliary cruiser at the start of the First World War. When peace returned, she was concerted to burn fuel oil before being renamed *Montroyal* in 1924 after further refitting. She was taken out of service in 1929.

27

The Wreck of the *Empress of Ireland*

In the middle of the afternoon on Thursday, May 28, 1914, the *Empress of Ireland* left Quebec on her return voyage to England. Her outward voyage from Liverpool to Quebec had taken six days with a total of 1,477 people on board, 1,057 of them passengers. In her holds were 252 gold bars worth five million francs.

The St. Lawrence River opens into a magnificent, broad estuary, but in spring the thermal contrasts between the river and the air cause thick areas of fog to form, which were partly responsible for the catastrophe. At around 01.45 on the morning of May 29, the *Empress of Ireland* was rammed on her starboard side by the *Storstad,* a 6,000 ton Norwegian coaler coming off the high seas towards Montreal. The collision took place roughly 5-6 miles from the coast of Rimouski, a small township on the south bank of the St. Lawrence.

The irony here is that both ships saw each other. So given the conditions, how was it possible for such a collision to occur? In readiness to reach the sea, the *Empress of Ireland* had just dropped her pilot off at Father Point where the pilot boat *Eureka* was waiting for her and there was a radio telegraphy station. The captain of the *Empress,* Henry Kendall, caught sight of the boat when the weather was clear. He stopped in his tracks and changed course. It was then that the fog came down, plunging the two vessels into darkness. On board the *Storstad,* the captain was sleeping, and it was the first officer who made the decisions that led to the collision.

Every vessel displays a red flare on the port side and a green flare on starboard. If a helmsman sees a red flare on a boat he is due to pass, he knows that the two vessels must pass to port and must also display the red flare. In this case, however, it seems that the first officer had a poor understanding of this manoeuvre and the fog prevented him from rectifying his course. Once the two ships came in sight of one another, Captain Kendall attempted to change his direction, but it was too late.

The *Storstad* had a reinforced stem, designed to break the ice in very cold climates, that protruded seven meters under the water; it tore the hull of the *Empress* with terrifying ease. Upon impact, the captain of the coaler put the engine into reverse, enabling his boat to disengage but at the same time precipitating the drama.

Although the *Empress of Ireland* had a sufficient number of lifeboats to disembark all the passengers and crew, the speed of the events and an unfortunate combination of circumstances prevented them from confronting the catastrophe. Water poured in through a 7 meter by 4 meter hole and then through the scuttles. In contravention of instructions, these had remained open. Almost immediately, it seemed that only the passengers on the upper decks could be saved. The liner's list quickly reached such an angle that it was only possible to launch five or six boats. Less than quarter of an hour after the collision, the *Empress of Ireland* sank in the icy sea where the temperatures never rose above 2°C, regardless of season.

The shipwrecked people were taken aboard the *Storstad,* but only 465 survivors were counted, among them Captain Kendall. The St. Lawrence had swallowed 1,012 people, 840 of them passengers. With the disappearance of one of its two finest ships, Canadian Pacific was estimated to have lost 10 million francs.

The inquiry placed responsibility for the accident on *Sorstad.* $300 million were demanded of her owner, but the sale of the coaler would net scarcely $175,000.

WHAT BECAME OF THE GOLD?

In the summer of 1914, Canadian Pacific dynamited the ship's hull to recover from her strongroom around $150,000 worth of gold ingots, two coffers worth $1,100,000, as well as the mail carried by the liner. Lying at the mouth of the great river, the hull of the *Empress of Ireland* was in relatively shallow water. She was subjected to a great deal of looting, but the looters had to be content with taking away objects or dismantling navigation equipment.

AFTER THE SHIPWRECK, OBLIVION

News of this shipwreck caused a great stir, but it did not last long. Why did this catastrophe not make a great and lasting impression as the wreck of the Titanic had done only two years earlier? Most likely because a ramming excites fewer fantasies and romantic notions than a collision with an iceberg, a perfect symbol of the forces of nature. It is also probable that there were far fewer celebrities on board and the aura of success that surrounded the passengers was less marked. But above all, the disaster occurred only two months before the outbreak of the First World War, the first act of which was Austria's declaration of war on Serbia on July 28. As well, at the beginning of August, France, Germany and Great Britain were involved in a conflict where the naval effort was characterized by the intervention of submarines, giving rise to new sense of excitement.

EMPRESS OF IRELAND

STEERAGE

In the 19th century, vast movements of migration took place, most notably to the United States. In one decade alone, 1810-1820, 34 million Europeans arrived in the New World. The first to leave their country to establish themselves on the other side of the Atlantic were the English and the Scottish. The Irish formed a large contingent following the Great Famine of 1846-1847. Germans and Scandinavians began to settle there in the 1840s. At the end of the century there was , the arrival of new communities from Central and Southern Europe. These emigrants were an undemanding clientele who were provided with the very mininum of space and service. It was because of them that the liner companies were able to make their crossings economically viable while all the while marketing the prestige of their first class accommodation. Several networks were established to channel the emigrants to German or British ports. Transat, too, eventually set up recruitment offices and chartered special trains to transport the candidates for exile to Le Havre. For the latter, the critical moment was the obligatory passage to Ellis Island, an island situated next to New York City. It was there, after a cursory medical exam, that the verdict was delivered: either they were admitted to the "Promised Land" or they were repatriated to their country of origin. The American

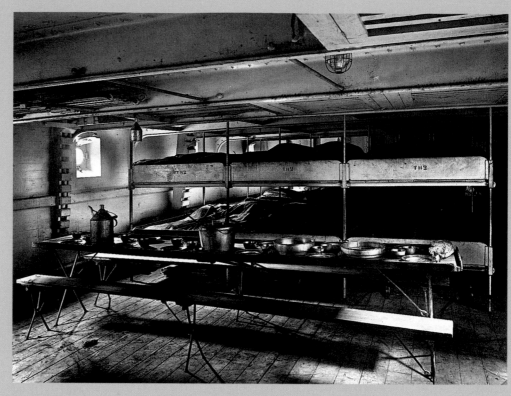

dream began to fade from 1921 onwards with the introduction of immigration quotas. The shipping companies embarked on an even more strenuous contest to attract the limited groups of would-be emigrants. In the 19th century the sanitary conditions on board were so deplorable that mortality rates were very high. Disturbed by this, the American authorities insisted on medical visits at the ports of embarkation. The increase in speed of liners, to 22 knots on average, reduced the length of the crossing and also made it possible to limit the number of deaths.

Above: Steerage on the Transat liner La Provence, which entered service in 1906. The previous year the USA had welcomed a million immigrants. The 808 third class passengers on La Provence were crammed into dormitories. They were not provided with blankets for fear they would make them into clothes.
Left: Emigrants on board NDL's Kronprinz Wilhelm.
Right facing page: On the bridge of HAPAG's Augusta Victoria.

Above: *The* Lusitania *in the port of Liverpool.*
Below: *The* Mauretania.

MAURETANIA
Length: 243 meters
(797 feet)
Width: 26.8 meters
(88 feet)
Tonnage: 31,938 tons
Speed: 26.75 knots
Passengers: 2,335
Crew: 812 men

LUSITANIA
Length: 239.9 meters
(790 feet)
Width: 26.7 meters
(88 feet)
Tonnage: 31,550 tons
Speed: 26 knots
Passengers: 2,165
Crew: 802 men

The Ocean Greyhounds

At the very beginning of the century, Germany prided itself on having the largest and fastest liners on the North Atlantic. The United Kingdom had lost the Blue Riband, as well as her prime position in the transportation of passengers on the Atlantic route to New York. On the latter, Cunard was the only large company which was completely British. The White Star Line was actually owned by the International Mercantile Marine (IMM), an American trust founded by Pierpont Morgan.

Exploiting national pride and the risk that Great Britain would lose its pre-eminence on the North Atlantic, Lord Inverclyde, Cunard's president, obtained a loan of 2.6 million pounds sterling from the British Government at a low interest rate (2.75%) for the construction of two transatlantic liners.

The construction of these liners, which originally were to measure 250 meters in length and 26 meters in width and to attain 25 knots, started in 1904 in two different shipyards: the *Mauretania* at Newcastle, the *Lusitania* at Clydebank, Glasgow. Their dimensions and tonnage were different, but any difference in their performance was accounted for mainly in the design of the propellers, with the *Mauretania* having blades six inches longer than those on her sister ship.

An Incomparable Line

It was in 1907 that Cunard delivered of the two ships, inaugurating the era of five day crossings between Europe and America. Externally, there were two features that distinguished each of the sister ships: the scuttles on the bridge of the *Mauretania* were square; the *Lusitania's* funnels appeared taller, because the decks were not encumbered with air vents, which were flat.

The first ship to take to the seas was the *Lusitania* on June 7. Two hundred thousand people watched her depart on her maiden voyage. It was the largest ship in the world until the *Mauretania* came into service on November 7 (the latter won the Blue Riband on her maiden voyage with a speed of 23.69 knots).

Nicknamed the "Ocean Greyhounds" as much for their speed as the purity of their lines, these liners were different in other ways; not only were their methods of propulsion different, but they also had interior fittings that were luxurious but nevertheless entrusted to different designers. The *Lusitania* represented the classicism typical of the era, resorting in the main to predominantly white stucco. This relatively spare style gave the impression of a somewhat lofty majesty. On the *Mauretania,* by contrast, the ambience was more welcoming, thanks to the greater use of wood sculpture and paneling. These liners were also the first to be equipped with an elevator for the first class passengers.

The *Mauretania* has earned her place in history having retained the Blue Riband for more that 22 years before yielding it to the NDL's *Bremen* in 1929. Except for a fire on board in 1921, she experienced no mishaps and enjoyed a long career that lasted until 1934.

During the First World War, the *Mauretania* was not converted into an auxiliary cruiser because of her huge size, although the Admiralty had imposed such a clause in the loan agreement with Cunard. Like the *Lusitania,* she remained on the commercial routes. But from June 1915 onwards, she undertook a small number of troop transports in Dardanelles operations, and served for a period as a hospital ship.

When peace returned, the *Mauretania* once again pursued her glorious career on the transatlantic route. After the fire in 1921, the opportunity was taken to change her engines to run on oil. On this occasion, her hull was repainted white. She was also used for cruises after 1930.

Although destined for an equally brilliant future, the *Lusitania* entered into legend when she became the victim of a torpedo attack on May 7, 1915.

33

The torpedoing of the *Lusitania*

At the start of the First World War, Germany boasted an enormous fleet of warships as well as a dozen submarines. On February 4, 1914, in order to break the British blockade, the German Imperial Government published a notice in the *Reichs-Anzeiger* which would weigh heavy for the remainder of the conflict. It declared the waters surrounding Great Britain and Ireland a war zone and gave notice that any neutral ship sailing in these waters did so at her own risk, and could be destroyed without warning.

This declaration brought about a protest from President Woodrow Wilson. The Germans replied by insisting on the dangers they ran because of the blockade and that the interests of the Empire were of paramount importance in their eyes.

On May 1, 1915, the German Embassy in Washington published an announcement in the *Ocean Travel* columns of American newspapers that was quite different from the other companies. Travelers on the North Atlantic route were reminded of the risk they took in entering the territorial waters of the British Isles. Two days later, the *Lusitania,* commanded by Captain William Turner, sailed out of New York port for England. On May 6, Captain Walter Schwieger, who commanded the German submersible U20, sank the *Candidate* and the *Centurion,* two ships belonging to the Harrison Company.

On May 7, the *Lusitania* was approaching the Irish coast. Although she was coming to the end of her voyage, it was now that the crossing became the most dangerous. Her captain was on a state of alert, as the German submarines had already demonstrated their destructive power, but he was somewhat reassured by the speed of which the liner was capable. The Germans considered a ship of such importance a threat since it could be converted into an auxiliary cruiser.

At 14.10 hours, the *Lusitania* was a dozen miles off Old Head of Kin-

sale, a cape close to the Irish port of Queenstown (the present day Cobh) in Cork. A single torpedo, launched without warning from Schweiger's U2, struck the starboard side of the ship and in twenty minutes the *Lusitania* sank. Only 764 passengers were rescued. Of the 39 children present on board, only four were put on lifeboats. In total, this rapid sinking claimed 1,198 lives. Among the victims were 124 Americans, of whom some of the celebrities in first class are remembered, most notably Alfred Vanderbilt, the Railroad King, who offered his lifebelt to a passenger who could not swim.

Captain Turner was one of the survivors, rescued after spending three hours in the water. In the inquiry following the catastrophe, he was reprimanded for not following Admiralty instructions for avoiding under water torpedoes. He had slowed down instead of maintaining maximum speed, come too close to the coast and had not followed a zigzag course.

The torpedoing of the *Lusitania* provoked extreme reactions on both sides of the Atlantic. While seen as a great naval victory in Germany, it aroused feelings of horror in the United Kingdom. At the same time, it stirred up an unprecedented wave of indignation in the United States, whose nationals were paying a heavy price for a war not of their making. It has often been suggested that this torpedo attack was what pushed the United States into the First World War. It would be more accurate to say that this savage attack, which took place without the customary warning, inflamed the opinion of a public which had regarded itself as neutral in this conflict even though, considering their origins, the majority of Americans were in favour of the Allies.

The United States' entry into the war was more the consequence of multiple attacks against civil vessels in the course of conflict, one of the principal features here being the in-

tervention of submarines. The sinking of so many merchant navy ships, notably American ones, could be compared in some respects to an iceberg in which the loss of the *Lusitania* was only the tip.

Obverse side: The circumtances surrounding the torpedo attack. The date of May 5 is a mistake.

Reverse side: A skeleton representing a Cunard ticket seller: "Business before everything".

The announcement of the torpedoing of the *Lusitania* was a major propaganda tool for the Imperial German Government, which had been waging war for nine months. The commemorate the event, a German patriot struck one hundred bronze medals. (See left). The British Intelligence Service made ample use of this initiative, turning it to their advantage. They had several thousand copies of this medal minted—probably 35,000 in all—in an alloy of poor quality, which was circulated among the British population, making it an instrument of anti-imperial propaganda.

34

THE TESTIMONY OF WALTER SCHWIEGER, THE U20 COMMANDER

"The overloaded or badly loaded landing craft were battered in the waves. The panic-stricken people climbed up and down ladders. Men and women jumped into the sea and tried to climb onto the capsized craft. It was the most awful sight in my life. I could not offer them any help. I could have rescued scarcely a handful of people. Furthemore, the cruiser we had just encountered could not have been far away and must have received distress signals. It might arrive at any moment. The spectacle was too awful to watch: I dived twenty metres and moved away."

Quoted by Lowell Thomas, The underwater Corsairs, Payot 1930.

CONSPIRACY OR DRAMATIC CHANCE

The loss of the *Lusitania* gave rise to the craziest of conjectures based on the hypothesis that the sinking was planned. An idea circulated that Winston Churchill, First Lord of the British Admiralty since 1911, had sanctioned it to draw the United States into the conflict, or that Captain Turner was in the pay of Kaiser Wilhelm II. None of these suggestions has ever been proven. Likewise, it has not been possible to identify the person who sent telegrams signed "Death" to certain passengers before their embarkation to warn them that the ship would be torpedoed. The theory of a German ambush does not stand up to scrutiny either. The *U20* came across her huge prey purely by chance.

THE SECOND EXPLOSION

How could a liner as important and well designed as the Lusitania sink in only twenty minutes, when the day before the U20 commander had sunk two ships, the *Candidate* and the *Centurion,* which had taken two hours and eighty minutes, respectively, to sink? On this occasion, a single torpedo had sufficed to sink the vessel. The Germans later claimed that the ship was transporting a cargo of explosives. If these had been loaded in contravention to international law, would this explain the second explosion that some of the survivors insist they heard? Underwater exploration of the hull has not been able to find any military hardware that would have explained the speed of the sinking. However, it would appear that the holds of the *Lusitania* were loaded with 4,343 cases of munitions, which the British authorities have since acknowledged. The most plausible explanation seems to be that the explosion was caused by coal dust. As it penetrated a bunker where most of the fuel had been removed for the crossing, the torpedo may have stirred up a cloud of coal dust which came in contact with the oxygen in the air and the torpedo flame, causing an explosion that opened an immense breach on the starboard side of the ship.

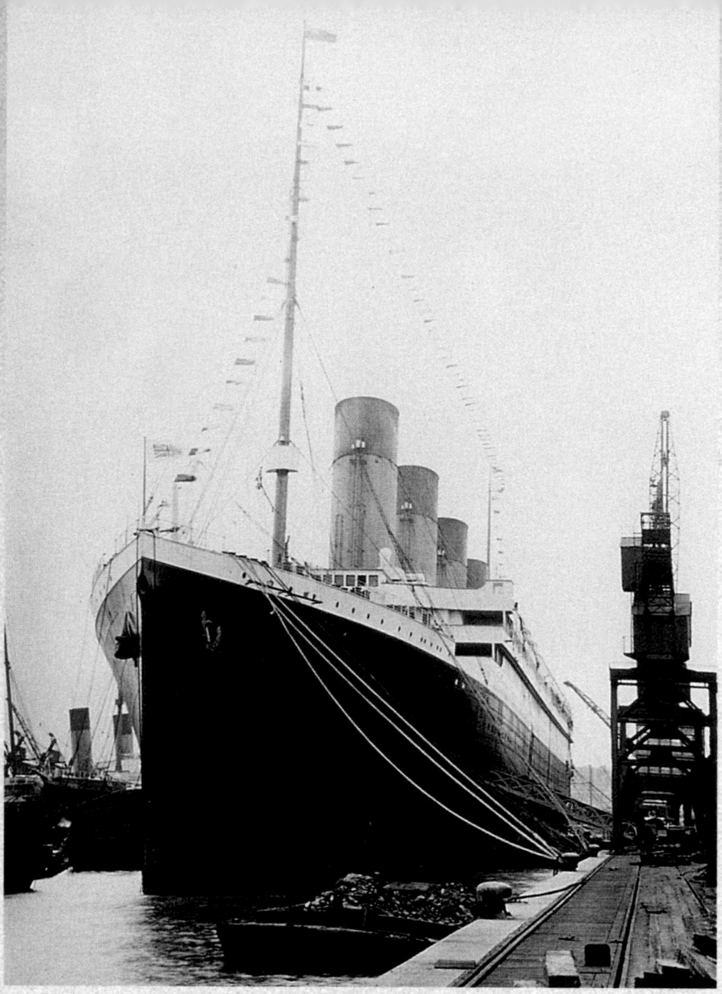

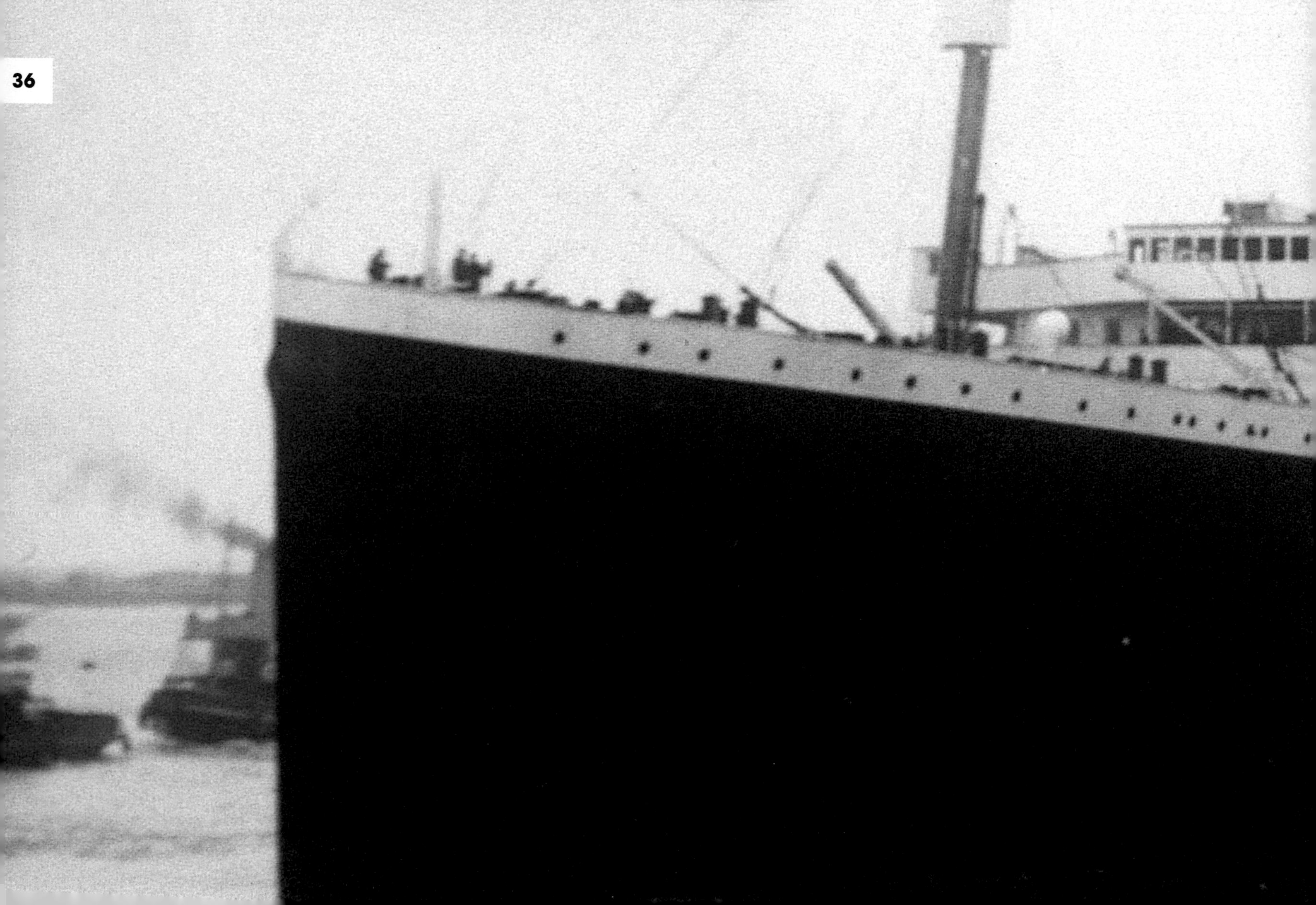

Three Sisters, Three Destinies

TITANIC
Length: 269.1 meters
(883 feet)
Width: 28.2 meters
(92 feet)
Tonnage: 46,329 tons
Speed: 22 knots
Passengers: 2,603
Crew: 900 men

At the end of the 19th century, White Star boasted faster liners than its British competitor. But with the appearance of the Cunard Line's "Ocean Greyhounds", the situation was soon reversed. So the company decided to order three monsters from Harland and Wolff. The first two would be built in the same dry dock in Belfast. Such an occurrence was unprecedented. The two giants took shape next to each other, thanks to a giant traveling crane which was a technological feat in itself.

The first of these liners, the *Olympic* was launched on October 20, 1910. It left on its maiden voyage from Southampton to New York under the command of Captain Edward Smith, who would also be the short-lived captain of the *Titanic*. She was then the largest liner in the world, beating the *Mauretania,* stretching over 268 meters long and weighing 45,324 tons. She retained this record until the *Titanic* was brought into service nine months later. As a result of the Titanic catastrophe, she stayed in dock for a long time for improvements to her safety, such as modifications to the watertight bulkheads caissons and an increase in the number of lifeboats.

Requisitioned in September, 1915, as a troop transport during the war, the *Olympic* resumed her career after the cessation of hostilities, once her engines had been adapted to use oil. The service she rendered over the next decade would earn her the nickname "*Old Reliable*", but at the beginning of the thirties, during a global economic crisis, her immense size proved to be a handicap which resulted in her being removed from the North Atlantic route to do cruises.

She was taken out of service in 1935, one year after the merger between Cunard and White Star, and one year before the appearance of the *Queen Mary.*

37

OLYMPIC
Length: 268.8 meters
(882 feet)
Width: 28.2 meters
(92 feet)
Tonnage: 45,324 tons
Speed: 22 knots
Passengers: 2,584
Crew: 860 men

AUCTION SALES

Similar to the *Titanic*, the *Olympic* boasted, in addition to a monumental dining room for first class passengers, a more intimate area called the "restaurant à la carte," equivalent to what is nowadays called a grill. In May, 1997, Sotheby's auctioned 80 meters of the panelling which had adorned this restaurant before being installed in an apartment in Southport, near Manchester, England. It had been bought in 1935 by a former mayor of the locality who had used it to cover his walls, with twelve workmen engaged on the project for at least a year. The next owner attracted by the decor was unaware of the origin of the panelling at the time of the purchase. She only found out much later after investigations by her son. As well, this decoration was sufficiently impressive to prompt a visit from James Cameron, the director who showed such concern for detail in his cinematic reconstruction of the sinking of the *Titanic*.

BRITANNIC
Length: 275.2 meters (903 feet)
Width: 26.75 meters (88 feet)
(as a result of a double hull over two-thirds of its length)
Tonnage: 48.158 tons
Passengers (in civilian use): 2,573
Crew (in civilian use): 950 men

THE BRITANNIC

The third sister, which went into service in 1914, was to have been called the *Gigantic*. But after the *Titanic* catastrophe, White Star's directors decided to offer proof of their humility. So they named her the *Britannic*, a choice colored by a patriotism that seemed to be welcomed in the troubled international situation that was unfolding at the time. The *Britannic* was to be more luxurious and larger than either of her elder sisters, but this extravagence was to never be fully realized. At the beginning of the war, she was converted into a hospital ship for over 3,300 wounded and was never to have a civilian career. On November 22, 1916, off the Greek island of Kea, she was sunk by a mine laid by the German submarine, the U73. Fortunely, however, the liner benefited from its reinforcement against the risk of sinking, most notably by the double hull. Her sinking cost the lives of only thirty people out of the 1,134 on board. The majority of the victims had embarked—without permission—on two launches which were subsequently destroyed by the liner's propellers. Moreover, those on board were all able-bodied, since the *Britannic* was sailing with technical and hospital personnel in search of patients at Moudros for repatriation.

Left: The Olympic, *and above, its first class restaurant.*
This page: top: The Britannic *as a hospital ship.*
Right: The cover of the Titanic Commutator, *the official revue of the Titanic Historical Society, and above it the owners of the wooden panelling from the "restaurant à la carte" of the* Olympic *prior to the auction.*

THE TITANIC COMMUTATOR
VOLUME 14, NUMBER 4, WINTER 1990
OLYMPIC'S RESTAURANT DISCOVERED

THE PIED PIPER OF HAMELIN

In the course of her long career, the *Olympic* was by turn victim, savior and persecutor. On her arrival in New York at the end of her maiden voyage, the *Olympic* drew a tug into her path which emerged badly damaged from the incident. On September 20, 1911, in circumstances that were never properly explained, the *Olympic* collided with the cruiser, *Hawke,* in the port of Southampton. The two ships suffered considerable damage and the cruiser nearly capsized once again, after taking on water. During the war, the *Olympic* was requisitioned as a troopship and took on passengers from the *Audacious,* a British battleship that had been badly damaged by a mine and eventually sank. On May 12, 1918, she managed to ram and then sink a German submarine that had tried to torpedo her. In May, 1934, a few months before being taken out of service, the *Olympic* sliced the *Nantucket* fire-boat in a dense fog, a catastrophe that resulted in seven victims on the stricken ship.

Such a Calm Night ...

On Wednesday, April 10, 1912, the *Titanic* set out from Southampton at around noon on her maiden voyage to New York, carrying 1,308 passengers and a crew of 885. She called at Cherbourg at Queenstown to take on Irish emigrants, and then took to the high seas in the late morning of April 12. The North Atlantic was hers.

The first days of the voyage showed no problems. On Friday, April 12, at around 19.45 hours, the *Titanic* passed the liner *La Touraine*, which had reported by radio the presence of icebergs. Two days later, five different ships alerted her of the same dangers and advised her to modify her course.

On Sunday, April 14, the liner was close to Newfoundland; on the south west tip of the island was Cape Race and its wireless telegraphy station. At around 23.40 hours, the watch on the *Titanic* reported an iceberg straight ahead at about 600 meters. Bearing in mind the speed of the liner, this distance would be covered in only a minute's time. Immediately her engines were put into reverse and the rudder was activated to turn the vessel to port. But the lead time was around 30 seconds, during which the ship charged straight towards the obstacle. She changed course but not sufficiently to avoid a collision. It was ice giant against steel giant, the 30 meter high mountain struck and scraped the starboard side of the ship with a shock that was hardly felt. However the ship listed immediately to an angle of 5°.

Summoned to survey the damage, Thomas Andrews, the ship's designer, quickly realized that the *Titanic* was doomed. The hull, built of the strongest materials, comprised sixteen compartments separated by watertight bulkheads. But the gash was too great, comprising six holes. Andrews estimated two hours was the longest the Titanic could survive before going under.

At 00.15 hours, the station at Cape Race received a distress signal from the telegrapher, Philips, indicating the position of the ship. Philips and his assistant, Bride, continued to send messages. These were received by other vessels as well, but which of them were close enough to the *Titanic* to consider changing direction? Only the *California*, which did not intervene, and Cunard's *Carpathia*, which was 58 miles away and did not arrive on the scene until four hours later.

The first lifeboat was launched at 00.45 hours, the last at 02.05 hours. At 02.20 hours, with its prow submerged, the Titanic lifted its poop vertically above the ocean and sank forever.

It was all over with no backwash; how calm the night would have been were it not for the cries of terror of the 1,500 or so people who did not find room on the lifeboats.

A terrible toll...

The disastrous sinking of the *Titanic* cost the lives of 1,503 people. Had the *Titanic* struck the iceberg head-on, without doubt she would have resisted the impact. By striking it sideways, however, she received a dagger blow that inflicted damage in six places.

Captain Smith wanted to prevent an outbreak panic among the passengers. The safety equipment amounted to 14 launches for 65 people, two others for 45 people and four collapsible dinghies.

The first launch to touch the water only took 27 people, and the crew of the Carpathia found one containing only 12 survivors. Even the last to be launched was occupied by only 36 women and children and four crew members.

How can such a mess be explained? Firstly, at the start of the evacuation the real danger was not revealed, so many women felt apprehensive about being separated from their husbands and going 30 meters down the side of the ship with their children at night in icy temperatures.

But it was also a consequence of treating men and women differently and a certain lack of organization in the conduct of the rescue. Some officers obstinately refused male passengers access to the launches; seven launches had not a single man on board except for the occasional crew members.

Though the life boats provided 1,178 places in total, the *Carpathia* picked up only 703 people: 367 women and children, 126 men, and 210 crewmen.

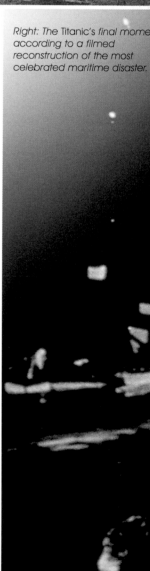

Right: The Titanic's final moment according to a filmed reconstruction of the most celebrated maritime disaster.

Above: The Titanic colliding with the iceberg as published in Le Petit Journal. This is an illustration produced during the initial excitement when contradictory reports were circulating. In fact, the Titanic did not strike the iceberg head-on, but scraped against it on her starboard side.

THE *CALIFORNIAN*...

On April 14, the *Californian's* radio sent the *Titanic* a message warning of the presence of icebergs. It was then rebuffed by Harold Bride, who was very busy transmitting to Cape Race the frivolous comments that the well-off passengers were telegraphing to their relations and friends. Towards midnight, when the *Titanic* was taking on water, the liner's officers saw the lights of a ship; to attract its attention they let off flares. Why did the crew of the *Californian* not react? The officers defended themselves by explaining that they had seen the flares, but the white lights did not correspond to any maritime conventions.

...OR MAYBE NOT?

Fifty years after the sinking, the officer of a *Norwegian* ship, the *Samson*, belatedly stricken with remorse, admitted that he and the other members of the crew had seen the flares let off by the nearby *Titanic*. Believing the flares to be from a customs vessel, the *Samson's* officers had decided to get out of territorial waters as quickly as possible.

41°46' NORTH, 50°14' WEST

02.20 hours on an icy cold night. More than 1,500 people were left off the rescue launches, had been hurt or killed by the collapse of a funnel, or tried to float in a desperate effort to get a place in a launch or raft, whose occupants had to ensure their survival by preventing overloading. Captain Rostron, who commanded the *Carpathia*, set his vessel on full power and, regardless of the danger, prepared to take on the survivors. When he arrived on the scene he found distraught survivors and floating bodies. Harold Bride, one of the *Titanic's* radio officers, immediately set to work to transmit a first list of survivors, despite his frozen feet. Later the messages from the *Carpathia* were remarkably succinct, fueling the concern among the families of the passengers. The *Carpathia* took three days to reach New York, arriving on the evening of April 12, berthing at the White Star terminal where the *Titanic* should have stood.

↓ 75 FEET FROM BOAT DECK TO WATER.

Colonel Astor

Forty-seven year-old John Jacob Astor was one of the richest men in the United States. His fortune was based on hotels, the flagship of which was the Waldorf Astoria.

But money could not buy everything, even in the land of the dollar. Following his divorce, the colonel was ostracised by American high society for marrying Madeleine Force, 20 years his junior. To escape from this indecorous situation, he took his new wife for a long tour lasting several months to Egypt and then France, hoping to reintegrate himself into the establishment when Mrs. Astor was five months pregnant. Although his new wife was able to find herself a place in a launch, Lightoller, the second lieutenant, refused access to the colonel. Astor did not insist, not wishing to take advantage of his influence to get on board, and the circumstances of his death served to rehabilitate his reputation in his country. His body was found a week after the sinking, mutilated by the collapse of a funnel. The dignity of his behavior earned him a funeral worthy of a hero.

Benjamin Guggenheim

This other millionare was known as the Copper King. He was returning to America after an escapade lasting several months in Europe with one of his mistresses. During the *Titanic's* sinking, he also behaved in an exemplary fashion. He wore a tuxedo—for if he was going to die he wanted to do so dressed as a gentleman - and went off to take part in the evacuation of the women and children. He entrusted this message for his wife to a steward, who was one of the survivors: "If anything happens to me, tell her that I did my duty right to the end." The message was delivered to Mrs. Guggenheim.

George Widener

This American millionare was known as the Tramway King. On April 14, he invited Captain Smith into the "restaurant à la carte" to celebrate the maiden voyage of the *Titanic and* its supposed unsinkability . He was travelling with his wife and son, Harry, an expert bibliophile who had just bought an extremely rare work by Bacon dating from the 16th century. The water swallowed up father and son, who no doubt went down clutching the treasure he had just bought. At least this was how he jokingly described the notion to the bookseller who sold him the work. The only survivor in the family, Mme. Widner, donated Harry's collection to Harvard University, where her son had studied. She also gave $3.5 million to build the library which bears his name.

Isidor and Ida Straus

He was the owner of Macy's, the largest store in New York. Ida was his loyal wife who refused a place in a lifeboat to stay with her husband. They had been together for so long that they could not imagine separation. Both sat side by side, clasping each other's hand and waiting for death. Mrs. Straus's portait was widely publicized in both the American and British press, when the tragedy prompted journalists to assign both praise and blame to passengers who either demonstrated heroism or spinelessness, according to their economic natures.

Major Butt

Aide-de-camp to President Taft, Butt was returning from Europe and carrying a message from the Pope addressed to the First Citizen of the United States. His disappearance in the disaster may explain to some extent the eagerness of the American Government to set up a commission when the *Titanic*, a British ship, had sunk outside American territorial waters. Apparently, Major Butt had taken an active part in the evacuation of women and children, only later returning to the smoking room to finish his interrupted game of bridge.

William Stead

The British owner of the *Pall Mall Gazette* was on his way to New York to take part in a peace conference, of which he was a firm proponent. During the whole crossing he was assailed with premonitions, forever casting doubt on the unsinkability of the *Titanic* to his fellow-passengers. When his fears were finally realized, he awaited the end in a smoking room with a cigar.

Edward Smith

Aged 62, Smith was the highest ranking captain of the White Star Line, which he had served for 32 years. During his career he had experienced neither collision nor shipwreck. Although attached to the *Olympic*, he was switched to the *Titanic* for the liner's maiden voyage. After the return journey, it had been decided that he whould take a well-deserved retirement. After the evacuation, during the ship's last moments, he absolved the crew of all reponsibility. "You have done everything possible," he said. "Now it is every man for himself." He would be one of the victims, but it remains unclear as to how he died. Some have claimed that he was drunk, but there are also stories of him committing suicide after accepting blame for the *Titanic's* demise. It is also ramored that he rescued a child and then disappeared into icy cold sea; and that his last words were, *"Be British,"* a remark which sums up to perfection an age and a country.

Thomas Andrews

The chief architect of the Harland and Wolff shipyard in Belfast was travelling on board the *Titanic* to note down all the teething troubles. This meticulous veteran recorded even the slightest weaknesses of the liner, from the standard of operation of the engines to the comfort of the passengers. The premature end to the voyage showed to what extent this stickler for detail showed his nautical myopia in believing in the unsinkability of the *Titanic*. As the ship sunk, Andrews must have realized that he had presided over the design of the greatest coffin of the age, and one that which would receive him in the end.

Bruce Ismay

The son of White Star's founder, Ismay was its president, even though the company's passing into the bosom of the Morgan Group had taken away a certain freedom of action. A passenger on board the *Titanic*, he jumped onto a life raft at the last minute, while hundreds of women and children were still waiting on the deck. Did he take someone's place? Did he save himself at the expense of someone else? It is difficult to be sure. What is clear is that at the moment the ship went down, panic seized the remaining passengers and that an "everyone for himself" mentality prevailed. In April, 1912, Ismay still had another 25 years to live, during which the memory of the disaster would haunt him constantly. His agony began with his return to New York, when he had to face the accusations of the commission of enquiry, and of the American and British press as well. The fact that he was numbered among the survivors was considered an obscenity. But he was criticized equally for having pushed the engines to the limit, if not to gain the Blue Riband then at least to make the *Titanic* a faster giant than her sister ship, the *Olympic*. Ismay never managed to absolve himself of the accusation. An investigation of the liner's hull in 1987 was able to establish the truth 75 years after the tragedy: the *Titanic* was sailing at a maximum of 20.5 knots at the time of the collision when the maximum speed of the ship was 22 knots. The president of White Star had not interfered in vessel's operation. Even so, he remained until the end of his life the scapegoat for the catastrophe. In 1913, he was forced to resign. The councils of two American towns called Ismay took steps to rename their localities. The deposed president finished his existence in gilded exile, forbidding anyone to mention the *Titanic* disaster.

John Pierpont Morgan

J. P. Morgan was an American banker who, after founding a railway and metallurgical trust, established a holding company, IMM, of which White Star was a notable contituent. Morgan was due to participate on the *Titanic's* maiden voyage, but feeling unwell at the time, he abandoned the idea. He heard news of the catastrophe at Aix les Bains. He himself was not spared by the American commission, which was presided over by Senator Smith, a fervent opponent of trusts. Morgan died in 1913 at the age of 76. Although his age accounted for his death to a certain extent, the attacks he endured as a result of the disaster certainly did not help him in the end.

The Navratil Brothers

These two young boys aged two and four, were probably the best known survivors of the *Titanic* catastrophe. They had been registered on the liner under false names and their father was one of the victims. Regarded as orphans, they elicited a great deal of sympathy as well as several offers for adoption. It was through the press that their mother, a singer living in Nice, recognized them and came to find them in New York. The children had been abducted by their father who was taking them to America to start a new life. Michel Navratil, the elder of the two brothers, is still alive in France. At the present time he is the sole male survivor of the catastrophe and the only French national.

The Musicians of the Orchestra in First Class

W. T. Bailey, R. Bricou (a Frenchman), F. Clarke, W. Hartley, J. Hume, G. Krins (a young Belgian violinist from the Ritz Orchestra), P. C. Taylor and J. W. Woodward all became the real media heroes of the catastrophe. Right until the very last moment did they continue to play on the deck.
But what did they play in those last minutes? Legend, of course, speaks louder than the truth. One idea that persists is that it was *Nearer, my God, to Thee;* more than likely, however, they were playing the ragtime melodies of the era and finishing their careers with the less evocative hymn, *Autumn*. Whatever the case, the hymn they are supposed to have played has sold millions of copies. The orchestra and the *Titanic* have become inseparable. Wallace Hartley's body was found about a week after the sinking. The orchestra's leader was still clutching his violin.

Reverend Brown

Aged about 25, this young Irishman with a talent for photography was still only a seminarist when he was offered a first-class passage on board the *Titanic*. He immortalized the ship and her passengers before landing at Queenstown, his photographic assignment completed. It is to Brown that we owe all the photographs of life on board the *Titanic* and of the ambiance of its departure (they were published in 1937 by *Weekly Illustrated*). When he became an ordained priest in 1916, he pursued a dual career in religion and photography. The British considered him one of the greatest artists in his craft.

John George Philips

The chief telegrapher sent out distress signals until the technical equipment failed. He managed to climb into a launch at the last moment, but died of exhaustion before the *Carpathia* arrived on the scene.

43

The Titanic under a sea of ink

Journalists played a considerable role in the events surrounding the sinking of the *Titanic*.

To begin with, there were the newspapers which fuelled the legend of an unsinkable liner. White Star's directors never claimed such superiority, although the press's compliments helped the ship to become profitable. But it was after the disaster that certain characteristics of the profession really came to the fore. In the confusion of the first news reports, the newspapers adopted different attitudes.

During the night of April 14-15, the vice-president of White Star in New York, Philip Franklin, received a telephone call from the Associated Press informing him of the *Titanic's* collision with an iceberg. Pushed by journalists to give details he did not possess, Franklin gave reassuring replies insisting that the ship was unsinkable.

The *New York Times* was the first to devote its front page to the disaster, not hesitating to rent an entire hotel immediately next to the port. By working with such urgency, nobody at the newspaper thought to leave out the advertisements for the return voyage of the *Titanic,* which was scheduled to leave again on April 20.

On Monday, April 15, Philip Franklin received another message that the *Titanic* was en route for Halifax, Nova Scotia, being towed by the *Virginian,* and that everybody was safe and well. He informed the press, the majority of whose representatives passed on the news.

All this contradictory news and the fact that the later lists of survivors were incomplete aroused the concern of those awaiting the arrival of close relatives, as well as public opinion. As well, the news of the catastrophe was displayed on the bulletin board in Times Square.

The *Carpathia* did not reach New York until April 18, before a crowd of 30,000 people from which journalists had been excluded. That did not matter, however, since they hired a tug to watch the event from the water.

While waiting for the ship's arrival, the journalists played on the fears of the general public by inventing imaginary facts to excite their readership.

The information transmitted by the *Carpathia* was really very fragmentary. Why? Because one of the radio operators from the *Titanic,* Harold Bride, had received a message from the *New York Times.* The editorial board had offered to buy the exclusive rights to his eye witness account. Bride received 750 dollars, the equivalent of 18 months' salary, for his story.

Below: The press found a money spinner in the wave of public frenzy by exploiting the catastrophe.

PREMONITION

In 1898, a short work by Morgan Robertson entitled *Futility* was published in Great Britain. The author of this novella imagined a liner, reputed to be unsinkable, going down in the middle of the night after a collision with an iceberg. The most surprising fact was that Robertson had named his boat *Titan*. This is a highly presumptuous name if we refer to mythology. The Titans were a divine race descended from Uranus and Gaia, who were struck down by Zeus as they tried to climb to the heavens by piling mountains on top of one another. It seems that the drive for giganticism, which affected White Star as much as HAPAG, the ship companies found expression in the name of their ships.
For its three monsters, White Star had chosen three very symbolical names: *Olympic, Titanic* and *Gigantic*.

INEQUALITY ON BOARD

Were the passengers treated differently according to the deck of the *Titanic* they were on? This sort of practice was very common at the time. Statistical analysis confirms this theory, when the percentage of survivors from each class is compared. 63% from first class survived compared with 41% second class, 38% third class. It is certain that the first class passengers were the first to be informed of the evacuation order and accorded more consideration; this explains why some men managed to find places in the first launches. All the children in first class were saved with the exception of one small girl. It is also true that the first lists of survivors sent from the *Carpathia* featured the clients that had paid the most.
The configuration of the ship also explains a lot of things. First of all, the lower floors of the ship were further from the upper deck, where the life craft were located. Moreover, in the third class areas the cabins accommodated four or six people of the same sex. Men and women were separated, some to the front, others to the rear of the ship. Families were not together, unless they occupied an entire cabin, and regrouping was difficult because the engines were situated between the two sleeping zones. The origins of the emigrants also explain some matters.
The Anglo-Saxons and the Scandinavians survived in greater numbers than the Slavs and Southern Europeans, who did not speak English and were less used to the sea.
Were the women and children in third class treated differently? This was certainly true as the ship began to sink. But thanks to the intervention of passengers and officers, the golden rule of "women and children first" was quickly applied. So Lieutenant Lightfoot was unyielding to the end, refusing men access to the lifeboats, including Colonel Astor, even when the launches had been put to sea without a full complement of passengers.
When all is said and done, the principal victims were male passengers, most notably those in second class, while the launches only took 367 women and children, 126 men and 210 crewmen.

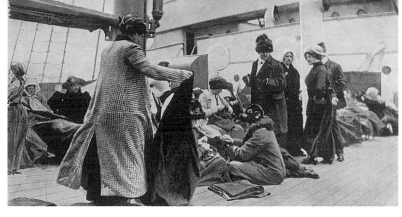

Adjacent: Survivors on the deck of the Carpathia. From their clothes we can see clearly that they are first class passengers who were more fortunate than the others.
Below: Sketches by a survivor of the different stages of the sinking.
Lower right: When the Carpathia had not yet arrived in New York and her telegraph operators were not very forthcoming, the press spread the the most varied rumors.

COULD THE ICEBERG HAVE BEEN AVOIDED?

The sinking of the *Titanic* was the result of a dramatic combination of circumstances. Her entry into service was initially delayed by a collision between the *Olympic* and the cruiser *Hawke* on September 20, 1911. In order to repair the sister ship, a certain number of parts had to be taken from the *Titanic,* which was then under construction. The liner would not normally have left on April 10 because a miners' strike that had severely compromised coal deliveries to liners. But as the *Titanic's* maiden voyage had been announced several months previously, in the eyes of White Star's directors it was essential for the ship to leave on time. To get round the shortage, coal was taken out of the bunkers of three other company ships in the port of Southampton. As a result of an exceptionally mild winter and spring, icebergs were drifting further south than usual. If the season had conformed to the norm, they would not have been found at such a latitude. Crows' nests of ship's are usually equipped with binoculars, but they were missing on the *Titanic.* Fleet, the lookout who spotted the iceberg, saw it when it was only 600 meters away. With binoculars, he would have detected it at a distance of 2,500 metres. The night of April 14-15 was notable for a total absence of air currents; wind forms a swathe of foam enabling lookouts to spot dangers from a distance. The radio messages sent by other ships warning of the presence of icebergs were not taken seriously enough. But the radio telegraphers were overburdened with work. Wireless telegraphy was a relatively recent invention and the first class passengers spent their time sending messages to their friends, as frivolously as if they were sending picture postcards. Captain Smith simply ordered a slight change of direction southwards without slackening speed. The blame was instead put on Bruce Ismay, the surviving president of White Star.

IT COULD HAVE BEEN WORSE

Curious though it may seem, the catastrophe could have claimed even more victims than it did. Firstly, the liner was only carrying 2,200 people, though her maximum capacity was 3,547 passengers. It was normal for a liner's occupancy rate to be relatively low for its maiden voyage. Many passengers preferred to travel on more veteran ships, whose teething troubles had been corrected following several crossings. Above all, the *Carpathia's* radio might never have picked up the *Titanic's* message, since her operator was about to turn off her equipment for the night. (At the time radio contact was not maintained for 24 hours a day, as wireless telegraphy was not yet being fully exploited at sea).

45

Above: the lounge
on the France.
Below: The France leaving
Le Havre for New York.
The destination flag
is on the forward mast
and that of the company
on the rear mast.
The postal flag is located
on the prow and the
national flag on the poop.

APRIL 1912: LAUGHTER AND TEARS

The *France's* maiden voyage began on April 20, 1912. Among her passengers were members of a delegation representing France at the inauguration of the statue of Champlain, the explorer who founded French colonies in the Great Lakes and St. Laurence regions at the beginning of the 17th century. The voyage took place when the world was still reeling from the shock of the *Titanic* catastrophe, where an insufficient number of lifeboats resulted in so many victims. The *France*, however, was the first ship in the world where the spaces of lifeboats exceeded the number of passengers conveyed.

A PRESTIGIOUS NAME

The liner put into service in 1912 is actually *France II*, since she was not the first Transat ship to bear that name. In 1865, the company had taken possession of an iron vessel, powered by paddle wheels, that was not taken out of service until 1910, after a long and very varied career. She provided service on several routes (Central America, New York, and the Caribbean) and had transported troops for military operations in Tonkin in 1884.

The Versailles of the Atlantic

Length: 217.2 meters
(696 feet)
Width: 23 meters
(75 feet)
Tonnage: 23,769 tons
Speed: 25 knots
Passengers: 2,020
Crew: 500 men

At her launch, she was the largest of the French liners, even though her dimensions and tonnage could not compare with the British and German giants of the time. The *France* was also the only French transatlantic liner to have four funnels. If she still occupies a glorious place in shipping history it is probably because of the magnificence of her first class accommodations, which earned her the nickname "the Versailles of the Atlantic" or "the Floating Paris". The sumptuous interior environment made her a great favorite with well-to-do Americans, some of whom were prepared to put in bids for the allocation of the de luxe suites, designed to accommodate up to six people. These had a private dining room, a lounge replicating one in a Tourangeau castle, and rooms equipped with four poster beds.

In the areas reserved for social activities, particularly noticeable was the grand staircase, a replica of the one in the Hotel Mazarin (National Library, Rue de Richelieu, Paris). It was the central pivot for a large number of lounges. The grandest of these, the conversation room in Louis XIV style, was adorned with impressive reproductions of celebrated paintings: one was a full length portarait of the Sun King by Rigaud, the original of which is in the Louvre, the other was a painting by Van der Meulen. There was also a Moorish salon, a reminder of France's imperial might. More intimate and with a lower ceiling, it was decorated with mosaics and Oriental carpets and provided soft divans. The deck was equipped—for the first time on a ship—with a skittle alley and a Punch and Judy show for children. The different first class decks were linked by an elevator, an item of equipment that was widely used in apartment blocks but a novelty on a French liner. In this respect, the *France*

provided the same conveniences as the *Mauretania* and the *Lusitania*. In the eight meter (26 foot) high dining room, service was at small tables, breaking with the tradition of large tables that were then in vogue. The cuisine held high the colours of French gastronomy and made its contribution to the general ambience of luxury on board. This liner was truly an ambassador of French refinement.

Requisitioned by the French Admiralty during the First World War, the liner served as a troop ship and naval hospital bearing the name *France IV.* At the end of hostitlities the giant continued her ambassadorial career for France until she was laid up in 1932.

REVEALING DETAIL

The *Imperator* was the liner with the largest tonnage of the age. It was also the longest, because in order to exceed the length of the *Aquitania* that was then being built, an eagle with the imperial crown on its head clutching a globe with its talons was attached to the prow. This obsession with records similarly recurs with a detail in the contruction of New York skyscrapers. For instance, it was because of its spire, which was purely decorative, that the Chrysler Building with its 318.8 meters (1,046 feet) was the tallest building upon its completion (just 40 meters more than the length of the *Imperator!)*

Above: the terrace of the former imperial suite on the Imperator.

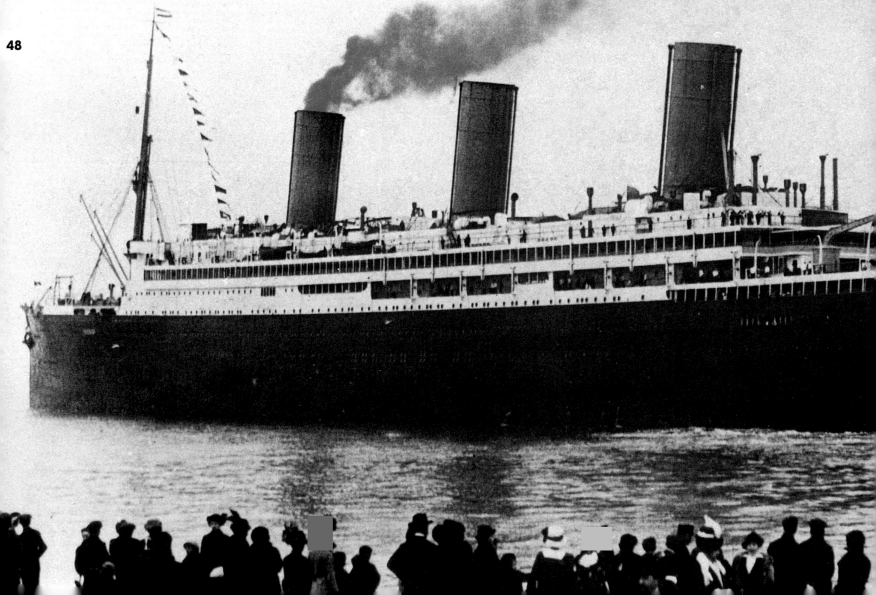

Length: 280 meters (918 feet) counting the imperial eagle which only survived two crossings before being detroyed in a storm; later 277.1 meters (909 feet)
Width: 29.9 meters
Tonnage: 52,117 tons
Speed: 24 knots
Passengers: 4,594
Crew: 1,108 men

A Mansion in Germany

In order to compete with the size of Cunard's and White Star's latest ships, HAPAG at the instigation of Albert Ballin, its president since 1902, placed an order for three liners of more than 50,000 tons in 1910. The first of these left the Vulkan Shipyards in Hamburg, and her hull was launched in 1912.

The *Imperator*, named in honor of Kaiser Wilhelm II, set off on her maiden voyage from Cuxhaven, becoming the largest ship in the world. The company, rather than concentrating on speed (the *Imperator* was designed to travel at 23 knots), placed their emphasis on comfort and luxury. The rooms were equipped with beds, not bunks, and the majority had bathrooms.

The wealthier passengers could even hire a suite with a veranda, including the service of personal servants.

Emphasis was also put on the decoration of public areas. The large lounge, 900 square meters (9690 square feet) in area, was decorated with wooden paneling, the ceiling embellished with a glass roof. High windows also looked out onto the starboard and port sides. At the end of the room, a bust of the emperor sat enthroned, wearing a helmet topped with an eagle. This symbol of power could also be found on the *Vaterland* the following year. In the evening, the same room was transformed into a ballroom, with seats and tables moved to the sides and the central space covered with a carpet adorned with foliage.

On the upper deck, the smoking room replicated the atmosphere of a large German mansion with a huge chimney, glazed bricks and wooden overhangs, and a ventilation system to remove the smell of stale tobacco. The first class dining room, which could accommodate nine hundred people, was decorated by Charles Mewes, who drew his inspiration from the London Ritz.

The most impressive feature on this ship was an astonishing swimming pool in Etruscan style, the first time a great liner was provided with one. Its measured 30 by 10 meters (100 feet by 33 feet), was decorated with columns and marble benches, tiles and mosaics, offered hot or cold water and incorporated a tepidarium and pool with gushing water. It was surrounded by 50 luxurious bathing huts on two levels, the upper level looking onto an enclosed gallery.

Though emphasis had been put on the ship's size and fittings, on its first crossing she showed a lack of stability, among other technical problems, causing the passengers some discomfort. However the *Imperator* was quickly modified to overcome these teething troubles.

The *Berengaria*

The career of this liner under the German flag was very short-lived, since she stayed in the port of Hamburg during the First World War. At the conclusion of hostilities, she served as an American troop transport before being handed over to Great Britain in 1920 as war reparations.

The following year she was sold to Cunard, who named it the *Berengaria*. The engines were adapted to run on oil and the ship was refitted to take only 2,700 passengers. She returned to service in May, 1922, but as her clientele on the North Atlantic route diminished, she was used for cruises in the Caribbean and Bermuda. In 1938 she was the victim of the fire that signed her death sentence, but her demolition was not carried out until 1946, following the end of the Second World War.

LINERS IN THE STORM

As we look back, we can see that the liners have not had exclusively civilian careers, and that military authorities have always viewed them as an auxiliary fleet in war operations. As early as 1854, during the Crimean War, the *Great Western* was used to transport the British expeditionary force. European colonial expansion served to confirm the leading role played by the merchant navy; this was especially the case in expeditions mounted by the French (Tonkin) and the British (the Boer War). Admiralties were also interested in converting liners into auxiliary cruisers, i.e., into battleships for surveillance operations. This military role was envisaged in the design of the ships, which made provision for reinforced ribs, munitions holds and watertight bulkheads. In return, the companies obtained subsidies which allowed them to partially finance their construction.

During the First World War, liners of large tonnage could no longer be employed as auxiliary cruisers, since their size made them too easy a target for German submarines. They were then used principally for troop transports after being camouflaged. Other liners served elsewhere as hospital ships for soldiers wounded in combat. These had the advantage of extensive decks on which a large number of beds could be placed. This enabled the most seriously wounded to be accommodated close to the life boats, should the ship be hit by a torpedo or a mine.

During the Second World War, a number of liners served again as troopships, like the valiant *Queens*. But governments requisitioned them for another purpose as well—to evacuate civilians. This was how Admiral Dönitz managed to embark a large portion of the population of East Prussia when threatened by the unstoppable Soviet advance. The British employed them in the same way, though they did not use liners to evacuate children after September 1940, following a torpedo attack on the *City of Benares* en route to Canada. The sinking caused great loss of life, and only seven of the 90 children were saved.

During the Second World War, Germany and Italy planned to convert their largest liners into aircraft carriers. The *Roma* was completely transformed for this purpose. But these plans were abandoned, since the air forces of these two countries had no planes capable of taking off or landing over such short distances. Meanwhile, this reconfiguration was carried out by the British—on two ships belonging to the Union Castle Line—and by the Japanese.

A few statistics will shed light on the dangers faced by the merchant navy during the First World War. It is estimated that during the four years of conflict the Germans sank 5,000 of the 8,000 ocean going ships, half of which were sailing under the British flag. Around 40% of the total tonnage was sunk in this way.

The camouflaged Mauretania in the First World War. In an effort to minimize the risk of a torpedo attack, camouflage was designed to break up the lines of the ship and disorientate submarine crews. In fact, the main trump card for defending very large liners was the combination of speed with the suggestion that they follow a zig-zag course to disrupt aiming operations.

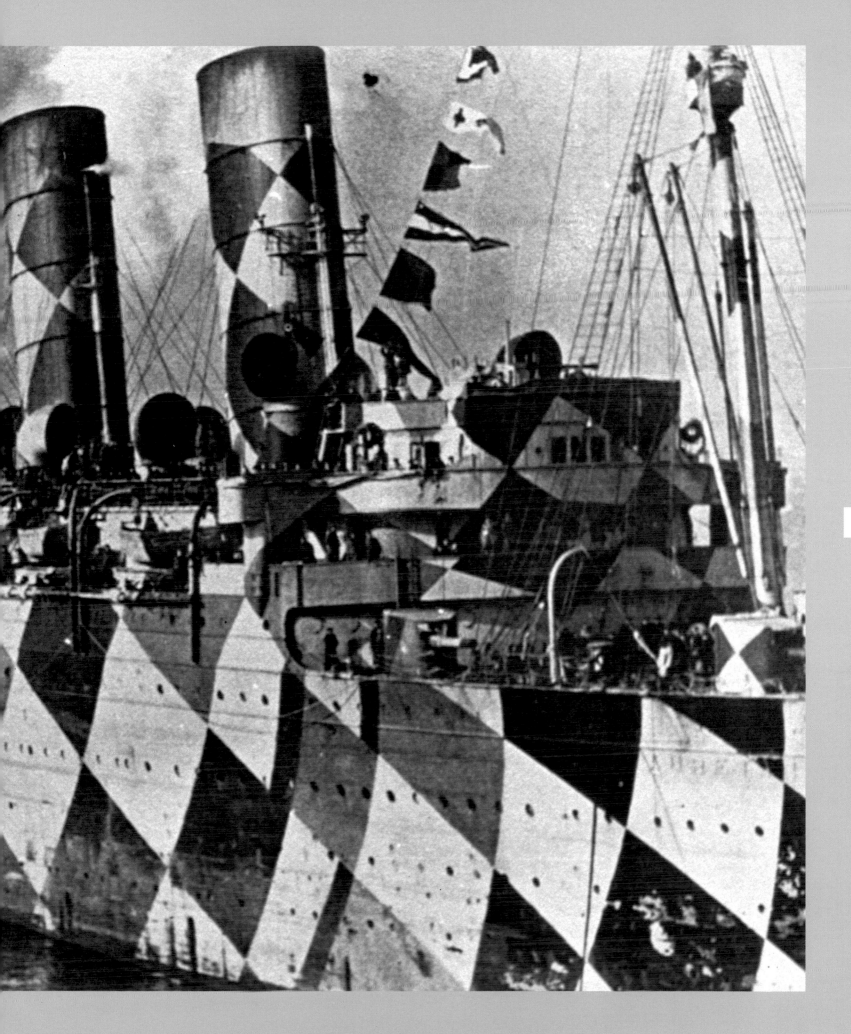

A Dinosaur in the Country of Men

The *Vaterland* was the second of the three giants ordered by HAPAG at Albert Ballin's request. Delivered in 1914, she was 12 meters (40 feet) longer than the *Imperator* and 2,000 tons heavier.

Her name, "Fatherland," illustrated the ambitions she roused both for the company's president, Albert Ballin, and in the mind of Kaiser Wilhelm II, who presented her with four 18th century Flemish paintings, a bronze figure of Marie-Antionette by Houdon and, naturally, a bust of himself as he had already done to adorn the *Imperator*.

When surveying the curious career of this monster, the most striking feature, however, is the extent to which her commercial performance differed from the hopes of her successive owners.

Disappointments

Her maiden voyage, which started from Cuxhaven on May 14, 1914, was a sorry affair. She arrived in New York a week later on tug power, since damage had occurred to the engines during the journey.

Many technical incidents followed, which meant that the *Vaterland* would only make a limited number of crossings before the outbreak of the First World War. From July 31 onwards, the ship stayed in New York. In light of repeated attacks by German submarines, the United States broke off diplomatic relations with Germany on February 3, 1917. On April 6 of that year, America declared war.

The previous night, the *Vaterland* had been seized by the American authorities. President Wilson hurriedly renamed it the *Leviathan*. Under this name, after seven months of preparation, it went back into service as a troop ship. Indeed, it was as a military vessel that the *Leviathan* gave the greatest satisfaction. Though the ship pitched and rolled in an unpleasant way, in one year she had transported a total of 100,000 American troops. Her reliability was much admired by the United States Admiralty. At the end of hostilities, the conversion of the *Leviathan* into a liner again took several years, since she did not take to the seas again until July 4, 1923, under the colors of the United States Lines. By that time she was already nine years old, for seven of which she had been inactive.

The remainder of the *Leviathan's* career amounts to a long series of disappointments for the directors of the company. This sad story can be attributed to a certain number of factors.

Firstly, there was the United States' new immigration policy that severely limited the number of entrants. The *Leviathan* had been designed to carry 3,350 people in second and third class. But how could one make a profit when the bookings were so greatly decreased?

By counting on first class passengers, perhaps? Not so. Since the Leviathan sailed under the American flag, she was considered an extension of national territory and as such was subject to the same laws, most notably those relating to prohibition, which remained in effect until 1933. For this reason, the wealthy passengers steered clear of the American ships, preferring the European liners where alcohol was served in abundance.

The end of a career

The world economic crisis which loomed in 1929 was the final reason that the *Leviathan,* whose operations showed huge losses, did not have the commercial success expected of her. The number of crossings that made a profit can be counted on the fingers of one hand. By contrast, it is impossible to count the number of breakdowns she experienced.

Her lugubrious final voyage between New York and the demolition yard at Rosyth, Scotland, serves to epitomized the *Leviathan's* whole career. She had no passengers for the crossing, the boilers stopped working one after another, seven fires were recorded in the engine room, and the crew threatened to go on strike.

Length: 289.2 meters (948 feet)
Width: 30.5 meters (100 feet)
Tonnage: 54,282 tons
Speed: 25.8 knots
Passengers: 3,889
Crew: 1,234 men

A PROPHETIC NAME

In deciding to rename the German liner *Vaterland* the *Leviathan*, Wilson made a great presumption. The name "Leviathan" is a Biblical reference which appears most notably in the Book of Isaiah: "On that day the Lord with his powerful and deadly sword will punish Leviathan, the wriggling, twisting serpent that lives in the sea." Hence, we conclude our history of this liner with the admission that the monster never succeeded in mastering the sea either technically or in terms of profitability. In any event, the choice of name was particularly unfortunate. To further prove this point, in the 19th century, Brunel had planned give the name *Leviathan* to his giant ship, later named the *Great Eastern*, whose erratic career also had commercial loss.

The largest ship in the world

S·S·LEVIATHAN
United States Lines
managing operators for
UNITED STATES SHIPPING BOARD

THE EXCEPTIONAL LONGEVITY OF THE *AQUITANIA*

Delivered on the eve of the First World War, the *Aquitania* was to have a long and glorious career, both as a merchant ship and a military vessel, until her sale in 1949, which led to her demolition the following year. During these 35 years, apart from conversions for military use, she had just one small overhaul in 1920 to adapt her enginess to run on oil, and another minor one in 1948. During her long life, she served in succession on the transatlantic route to New York, on military operations in the Mediterranean, on the emigrant transports to Canada, on the commercial route from Southampton to Halifax, as well as on luxury cruises for first class passengers in 1932.

FUNNELS ON LINERS

As time passed, funnels increasingly became a symbol of prestige and national power, to such an extent that on a number of ships, the *Titanic* for instance, one can find dummy funnels. It was the Germans with *Kaiser Wilhelm der Grosse* who pioneered this new shape, a visible manifestation of the shipping companies' race for speed. In total, twelve large liners on the Atlantic run were given four funnels each: five were of German design, six came from British shipyards and one was French. Two other four-stackers plied the route to South Africa, flying the flag of the Union Castle Line.

The faithful sister

Length: 274.8 meters (901 feet)
Width: 29.6 meters (97 feet)
Tonnage: 45,647 tons
Speed: 24 knots
Passengers 3,000
Crew: 972 men

Nicknamed "the ship of beauty" for her balanced lines, the Aquitania was the last of the great transatlantic liners to have four funnels.

Upon the delivery of this ship in 1914, Cunard strengthened its fleet on the North Atlantic route with this vessel based on the *Mauretania* and the *Lusitania.* Yet the *Aquitania* illustrated a change in the company's designs and foreshadowed trends that would assert themselves in the inter-war years.

Launched in 1913 and intended to compete with White Star's *Olympic,* the *Aquitania* was an even larger liner than her sisters and capable of 14 knots. Cunard had nevertheless given up competing for speed, which had led to high running costs. The company aimed to improve profitability by putting the accent on comfort and luxury, and also devoting more space to less wealthy customers and the transport of freight.

Designed to transport 3,230 passengers the *Aquitania* set out on her maiden voyage on May 30, 1914. Because of the amount of time she had spent in dock for necessary adjustements, she only managed three round trips before the outbreak of the First World War.

Noted for her very balanced design, the *Aquitania* had a long career, both civilian and military, in the course of which her reliability never failed. She was one of the rare liners to be spared a refit, since no major catastrophe or technical defect made it necessary. For this reason, she deserves a special mention.

The *Aquitania's* military career

When war was declared, the British Admiralty converted the *Aquitania* into an auxiliary cruiser, but she was too visible a target and consumed large amounts of fuel. A month later, the military authorities decided to use her for missions more suited to her size. She served first as a troop transport, but was later converted into a hospital ship in the Mediterranean for operations in the Dardanelles. With her 4,200 passengers, she was the largest hospital ship ahead of the *Britannic,* which could accommodate 3,300 casualties. Between 1917 and 1919, she was employed as a troop ship for American soldiers.

The *Aquitania* was the only superliner to play a military role in two world wars. In 1939, she was used once more as a troop transport. At the end of hostilities she repatriated American and Canadian troops, as well as transported British girls who were engaged to soldiers the other side of the Atlantic.

THE APOTHEOSIS

Over a short twenty year period, the world of the ocean liner would change a tremendous amount. The First World War had altered the context in which the merchant fleet was evolving, but the Treaty of Versailles did not consolidate the situation. Liners became an instrument of national pride, in particular with countries that would become dictatorships. Germany and Italy won renown in the conquest of the Blue Riband. For Germany, it was a way to hold up her head and become reintegrated in the concert of nations, before the chaos that the arrival of Hitler heralded. Mussolini, master of the game in Italy from 1922, saw in liners a brilliant demonstration of the advantages the policies of a Fascist regime could provide. The democracies of old Europe made up for the loss of trade, due to a falling off in emigrant numbers, with increasingly conspicuous luxury. Everywhere, the floating cities became true ambassadors of the ocean with an aesthetic elegance that carried to its highest degree what became known as "the ocean liner style," and was exemplified in the splendour of the *Normandie, Bremen* and *Nieuw Amsterdam.*

The "Aristocrat of the Atlantic"

In 1913, Transat commissioned a new liner for the North Atlantic route. The *Paris* was still on the slipway when the Great War broke out. To free the shipyard for military vessels, the hull was towed away to Quiberon. The building of the ship was not completed until 1921. On her maiden voyage to New York on June 15, the captain welcomed Marshal Foch on board the ship that was then the largest of the French liners.

As her entry into service corresponded to the period of euphoria that followed the end of the war, the *Paris* was much appreciated by American passengers. People had a very good time on board because the were no restrictions due to prohibition. This became even more so after 1929, when a terrace cafe was inaugurated on the 130 meter (406 foot) long promenade deck.

She was also the first liner—from 1929 onwards—to provide a dance hall where passengers could move around on the luminous floor of glass tiles that were lit from below.

When we compare the *Paris* with Transat's other liners, we find that she too offered luxury and comfort and yet she was very much a transitional vessel that preceded the more pronounced personalities of the *Ile de France* and, above all, the *Normandie*. We can see the first manifestations of the Art Deco style in the deluxe cabins, yet the dining room for 540 was more influenced by the taste of la Belle Epoque, with its heavy glass mirrors and extensive wrought ironwork, depicting flower and fruit motifs.

A career terminated at its zenith

Damaged in 1927 in a collision that resulted in the deaths of twelve people aboard the cargo boat she had rammed, and then again 'the following year by a fire which necessitated a complete overhaul, the career of the *Paris* was peppered with technical incidents. In addition to this, the liner suffered from her position in the Transat fleet between her two more prestigious sisters, the *France* and the *Ile de France,* which enjoyed a much greater reputation for excellence. However, this did not prevent the American from nicknaming her the "Aristocrat of the Atlantic." She served mainly on the Le Havre-New York route, but she was also used for cruises in the Caribbean and Mediterranean. In 1938, plans were made to put her just on this latter service, now that the *Normandie* had come into service three years earlier.

In 1939, the *Paris* died in full glory when she was given the task of transporting art collections across the Atlantic for the World Exhibition in New York. On April 18, a fire broke out in the bakery. Unbalanced by the quantities of water entering from one side, the *Paris* capsized the next day. For years, the people of Le Havre were forced to endure the sight of her overturned hull, port side up, her masts severed in order to enable the *Normandie,* blocked in drydock, to leave the harbor. Three years later, the *Normandie* herself was destined to suffer the same fate as the *Paris.* The hull of the *Paris* was not demolished until after the end of the Second World War.

Length: 234.15 meters (768 feet)
Width: 26 meters (85 feet)
Tonnage: 34,569 tons
Speed: 21,8 knots
Passengers: 3,233
Crew: 662 men

Left: A crowd rushes into the port of Le Havre after the Paris capsizes.

THE MARRIAGE OF AIR AND SEA

On May 21, Lindbergh achieved the first air crossing of the Atlantic aboard the *Spirit of St Louis.* This flight was the start of an amazing expansion. On June 6, *Miss Columbia,* piloted by Clarence Chamberlain, touched down at Eisleben, Germany from New York. On June 29, under the orders of Commandant Byrd, the conqueror of the North Pole, a crew embarked on the *America* to fly the first air mail route between America and Europe. The flight took place in wretched weather conditions and was not completed as planned at Le Bourget on June 30, but the following day at Ver sur Mer, in Calvados after a catastrophic landing. Nevertheless, the link had been established, thanks in large part to the crew of the *Paris,* with whom the crew of the *America* had kept in radio contact, assisting them by giving their position on several occasions.

BOBBIN ON THE SEA

Among the many passenger facilities, the *Paris* boasted a real cinema theater. The *Patria,* belonging to the Fabre Company, which entered service in 1914 on the Naples-New York route, had been the first to have such a facility. But the *Paris* went further in setting aside a specific room for the theater. The custom of film shows on board began with the *Deutschland,* this was merely a portable screen that was set up before the performance.

A SHORT LIFE

Several factors serve to explain the brevity of the *Majestic's* commercial operations. First of all, she was completed in Hamburg when Germany had already been vanquished. Given the financial situation of the country and supply difficulties, as well as the prospect of surrendering the vessel as war reparations, the materials used to finish her were not of the best quality. Hence the *Majestic* found herself handicapped when she entered service. As well, the British always preferred ships that were built in their own shipyards. White Star's directors took possession of the ship as compensation for the losses they had suffered in the conflict, most notably the loss of the *Britannic*. They did not view her as a replacement of identical worth, but merely as a stopgap. In these circumstances, it is not surprising that this unloved liner finished her career when the prestigious *Queen Mary* entered service.

Spanning the Inter-war Period

Length: 291.4 meters
(956 feet)
Width: 30.5 meters
(100 feet)
Tonnage: 56,551 tons
Speed: 23.5 knots
Passengers: approx.
2,150
Crew: approx. 1,000 men

After the *Imperator* and the *Vaterland,* the *Bismark* was to be the third and largest liner, intended to ensure HAPAG the leading position on the North Atlantic.

However, this vessel, which was due to enter service in 1915, was never to sail under the name the Germans had chosen for her, and would never be their flagship.

Indeed, when the Great War broke out, her construction was not yet finished and she stayed in dock in the Blohn and Voss Shipyards in Hamburg until the end of hostilities.

The Treaty of Versailles awarded her to the United Kingdom. The British Government then sold her to the White Star Line, and it was under the name *Majestic* that she set off on her maiden voyage from Southampton on May 10, 1922. Stretching 291 meters in length, she was the largest liner in the world at that time. She had this distinction until 1935, when the *Normandie* went into service.

The *Majestic* was not designed specifically to carry emigrants. This commercial decision was to prove a trump card in view of the immigration restrictions decided on by the American authorities. Instead, she was designed to carry around 2,150 passengers: 750 in first class and 850 in third class, with a crew of around 1,000. She was suited to a clientele of average means, comprising teachers, students and veterans returning to the battlefields of Europe. She also enabled immigrants to make the trip back in better comfort within the framework of East Bound—a seasonal return for financial reasons.

However, the *Majestic's* career as a merchant ship was short. In 1936, her owners handed her over to a demolition contractor. The latter then sold her on to the British Navy, which used her as a training ship under the name *Caledonia.* She would have no doubt taken part in the Second World War as a troop transport, had her fate not been sealed on September 19, by an accidental fire that caused her to sink at Rosyth, Scotland, where the British Admiralty had stationed her.

61

Above: The Roma.
Below: The Augustus
casting off. The color of
the hull of this ship, black
or white, varied according
to whether she was
engaged on crossings
or cruises.

The Empire, on the March

ROMA
Length: 216.1 meters
(708 feet)
Width: 25.2 meters (87 feet)
Tonnage: 32,583 tons
Speed: 24 knots
Passengers: 1,675
Crew: 510 men

AUGUSTUS
Length: 216,6 meters
(710 feet)
Width: 25.2.meters (87 feet)
Tonnage: 32,650 tons
Speed: 20 knots
Passengers: 2,210
Crew: 500 men

Built in the Ansaldo Shipyards near to Genoa for the Mavigazione Generale Italiana, the *Roma* and the *Augustus* were to strengthen the Italian fleet on the North and South Atlantic routes. They differed in the colors of their hulls: white for the *Roma;* black, then white for the *Augustus.* There were two other significant differences: their means of propulsion and the nature of their clientele. While the *Roma* worked by steam, the *Augustus* had a diesel motor. The latter no real innovation, however, since the Swedish liner, *Gripsholm,* had been equipped with such a motor in 1925— and it was a big challenge (yet successful) to have such technology on such an important ship. The *Augustus,* however, was the largest diesel liner of the day.

Another difference was in the layout of the cabins, which were divided into three classes. The *Roma* offered more luxurious fittings and was designed to accommodate 375 passengers in first class, 600 in second, and 700 in third. In comparison, the *Augustus* provided 302, 504, and 1,404 places, respectively. Similarly, however, the decor of he two ships was inspired by Italy's finest hours, with the opulence of the most expensive cabins, and the presence of a lido deck and a swimming pool between the two funnels. These latter features, peculiar to Italian liners, would be reinforced on the *Rex* and the *Conte di Savoia.*

From the Sea to the Ocean

The *Roma,* launched on January 26, 1926, entered service on September 21 of the same year; the *Augustus* started her commercial career the following year. Slightly longer than her sister ship, the *Augusta* was the largest liner of the time until the appearance of the *Rex.* Both spent their commercial careers on the Atlantic on the routes to New York and La Plata. In 1939, in view of the imminent conflict, there was a plan

devised to fit the *Augustus* with turbines to give her a greater speed than a diesel engine. This plan floundered, however, and in 1940 both ships were immobilized.

The *Roma* and the *Augustus* had parallel destinies in the Second World War. The Fascist authorities decided to convert both ships into aircraft carriers, an operation that was continued by the Germans after the Italians capitulated. The overhaul of the *Roma* was almost complete, but the ship, renamed the *Aquila,* would never be used as an aircraft carrier. Meanwhile, the work of converting the *Augustus* was halted at an early stage.

The unsuccessful military career of both ships ended in Genoa. For the *Augustus,* the end came in September 1944 as the result of sabotage by the Germans, who were trying to block the harbor. For the *Roma,* it began with a bombing attack by the Allies in 1944 and was completed in April 1945 by Italian frogmen, whose mission it was to prevent the wreck from blocking the harbor.

63

The Atlantic Peace Road

From the time she entered service on June 22, 1927, the *Ile de France* enjoyed great popularity with her clientele and her crews. She was the precursor of a very personalized "ocean-liner style," both in her shape and her fittings. Neither speed not size influenced her design; instead transat's directors aimed for luxury, comfort and modernity.

At the height of the prohibition era, her bar (which was 9 meters/30 feet in length) was nicknamed "the longest bar of the Atlantic." Her great staircase was resolutely Art Deco, a novelty on a French liner. There was also, for the first time, a chapel and a boxing ring. The panoramic "*Cafe de Paris*" overlooked the sea on three sides. The dining room, designed by Pierre Patout, had walls that were covered with marble, 8 meters (26 feet) high and lit by 112 Lalique wall lights, and was embellished with a fountain. The most luxurious apartments took the names of famous castles in the area around Paris.

This liner remained incontestably associated with luxury, but also with aviation. Indeed, from its deck the first sea plane was launched to shorten mail delivery times. As well, Robert Esnault-Pelterie, inventor of the joystick and and a pioneer aircraft builder, was married on board in 1928.

After an excellent record of service in the Second World War, the liner returned to civilian life on October 22, 1946. The work she underwent the following year resulted most notably in the removal of one of her funnels. She returned to the North Atlantic route to finish a long career that casted 32 years. But it was not for her longevity that her name stays in the memory.

The Saint Bernard

The *Ile de France* made her mark on history for saving so many people, earning herself the nickname "the St. Bernard of the Atlantic." During the war, she picked up the occupants of liners sunk by German submarines, and after the conflict she saved the wounded or the sick that were isolated on ships taht had requested assistance.

Her reputation was gained particularly from her mass rescues. In 1951, she escorted the British cargo ship, The *Cheswick,* before the latter was taken over by another ship. On September 21, 1953, in a full-force hurricane she picked up 24 of the 26 crew members of the Liberian cargo ship, *Greenville.* But she achieved her true glory following the sinking of the *Andrea Doria* on July 25, 1956. The captain, Raoul de Beaudean, had the idea of lighting up the *Ile de France* as it approached the stricken ship to offer hope to the survivors. He picked up 753 passengers, thanks to a well-controlled rescue operation. The *Ile de France* continued her career on the same route until 1959, when under Japanese ownership she went to demolition yards in Osaka. The report of her consignment to the scrap heap aroused a storm of protest, but it was not enough to prevent the fatal outcome.

Length: 241.3 meters (791 feet)
Width: 28 meters (92 feet)
Tonnage: 43,153 tons
Speed: 24 knots
Passengers: 1,786
Crew: 800 men

Below: Intended for advertising by travel agencies, this picture of the Ile de France is taken from a painting by Albert Sebille. The artist worked on the picture before the ship had completed her trials, but in reality the Ile de France did not possess such imposing air shafts.

A RECORD OF MEDALS

The *Ile de France* won the most medals in all of shipping history because of her service record in both war and peace. Most notably, she received the Croix de Guerre with distinction for her performance during the conflict, mainly in the Indian Ocean where she transported 40,000 soldiers and picked up survivors from countless ships torpedoed by Nazi submarines. She was also awarded the Croix de Chevalier de Merite Maritime after rescuing survivors from the *Andrea Doria*. In addition, the newspaper *Il Tempo* had a medal minted in her honor, subscribed to by its readers.

THE THREE TRIUMPHS OF THE *ILE DE FRANCE*

Traditionally, a liner's maiden voyage gives rise to expressions of welcome—a concert of sirens from ships in the ports of departure and arrival, and a procession of tugs and fireboats activating their water hoses. The crowd takes part in the celebration waving flags and handkerchiefs, and airplanes are also involved, flying over the newly enthroned vessel. The *Ile de France* was the only liner to receive such a triumphal welcome on three occasions when arriving in New York: after her first crossing in 1927; in July, 1949, after the work which returned her to civilian service; and on July 27, 1956, when she docked at Pier 88, reserved for the French Line, with the 153 *Andrea Doria* survivors on board.

MEALS AT SEA

Meals had always been essential times for first class passengers, if only because they broke up the long journeys and helped people to forget the time that often passed very slowly.

It was Transat that raised meals to the rank of great art on the liners. The company that gave up competing for speed preferred to attract their clientele by placing emphasis on the attractiveness of life on board and by perpetuating the French gastronomic tradition. In 1912, the *France* had introduced service at small tables. This modification would lead to the institutionalization of the captain's table. Originally, the captain was a technician. With the progress of steam, his role evolved to become the chief organizer of social activities. Nicknamed "the pasha," "my uncle" or the "mainmast" by the crew, at the suggestion of the chief steward and recommendations from the company management,

the captain had to arrange the delicate business of choosing which important people to invite to his table (except on the first and last evenings). On most days, the captain's dinner was a grand exercise of social virtuosity. Raoul Beaudean, who was captain of the *Ile de France* at the sinking of the *Andrea Doria*, summed up his duty perfectly in the title of his memoirs: *A Diplomat in Navy Blue.* Arthur Rostron, who captained the *Carpathia* and continued his career on the *Mauretania*, appreciated his public relations in moderation. For him, there were three sides on a liner: the starboard side, the port side and the social side. Some captains delegated this part of their activities to a steward whose table was similarly prized. But as a general rule, most took very much to heart a duty that flattered certain passengers whose loyalty added to the prestige of the company.

WHAT'S BRED IN THE BONE WILL OUT IN THE FLESH

The captains of different ships have told this story so often that nobody knows on which liner it originally took place. When organizing the captain's table, a steward suggested the inclusion of a couple of upstarts. The captain was hesitant, but eventually accepted them, bearing in mind the pasengers' wealth and their loyalty to the company.

The invitation ended in a rare rejection. "We pay a lot to avoid having to eat with the staff," they replied disdainfully.

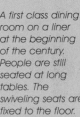

A first class dining room on a liner at the beginning of the century. People are still seated at long tables. The swiveling seats are fixed to the floor.

Dining room
on the Atlantique.

First class dining room
on the Flandre.

DIPLOMATS AT SEA

Put on the La Plata route, the *Cap Arcona* served the same route across the South Atlantic as the *Atlantique*. On her maiden voyage, the two ships passed. The captain of the *Cap Arcona* sent a long and very warm message to his counterpart in which he expressed his hope that the sea would bring the nations together. The equally benevolent reply insisted on the need for peace in Europe. Ironically, these pious wishes were nullified by two events in 1933. After leaving Pauillac Trompeloup, near Bordeaux, France for Le Havre on January 4, the *Atlantique* was destroyed by a fire in the English Channel the following day. On January 30, elections to the German legislature brought Hitler to power.

Length: 205.9 meters
(675 feet)
Width: 25,7 meters
(84 feet)
Tonnage: 27,560 tons
Speed: 21 knots
Passengers: 1,315
Crew: 630 men

Below: The Cap Arcona in the port of Santos, Brazil at the start of her career. She is flying the flag of the Weimar Republic on the stern mast.

Liberty minus five days

While the Germans were interested in the North Atlantic routes from the end of the 19th century onwards, they also had prosperous shipping companies serving South America. This subcontinent, which was a traditional area for German, had settled a clientele of rich planters who were perfectly willing to spend their money on pilgrimages to their country of origin.

The Hamburg-South America Line had already put the *Cap Trafalgar* into service on this route in March, 1914, and the *Cap Polonio* as well. The former was sunk in September, 1914, by the Cunard ship, *Carpathia*, in use as an auxiliary battle cruiser; the latter was handed over to the British authorities as war reparations in 1919, only to be bought back by the company in 1921. It remained in service until 1931.

The *Cap Arcona,* which set out on her maiden voyage on November 19, 1927, took over a route that was very profitable. Designed to sail at a cruising speed of 21 knots, the *Cap Arcona* was perfectly suited to the clientele she was targeting—wealthy colonials and emigrants. She was a fast and luxurious vessel that provided a limited number of space: 272 in first class, 272 in second and 465 in third. She was the first liner to have a regulation size tennis court on deck, located behind the third funnel.

In regard to luxury and size, she was far ahead of the British ships on this route. Only the Italian liners surpassed her, as did the *Atlantique* from the autumn of 1931 until her fire in January 1933. Right through the course of her civilian career, *Cap Arcona* carried wealthy passengers with little concern for expense, and who were prepared to hire inside cabins to store the goods they had bought in Europe.

The war years

In 1940, the *Cap Arcona* was requisitioned at Gdynia, where she served as a barracks ship. She remained there until the beginning of 1945, when she took part in the evacuation of German nationals from East Prussia who were fleeing the Soviet advance. In three trips, she transported some 26,000 passengers.

In April, 1945, she effected the evacuation to Lubeck of 5,000 prisoners from the Neuengamme concentration camp on the River Elbe, close to Hamburg. On May 3, after Hitler had committed suicide and Admiral Dönitz had taken over the reins of an exhausted war machine, the Royal Air Firce bombarded her in the bay of Lübeck. The ensuing fire created havoc among the occupants, who numbered more than 6,000 (prisoners, crew and guards). There were around 5,000 victims in this carnage, but no one is sure of the exact number.

On May 8 Germany capitulated.

BREMEN

Germany Regains the torch

Entering service in 1929, the *Bremen* symbolized Germany's economic revival after emerging from the First World War in ruins.

In 1926, NDL placed an order for two large liners that would be extremely fast and luxurious and define the Art Deco style according to German trends. The company's spectacular recovery had been made possible by agreements signed with American companies.

The name of the first ship to be completed, the *Bremen,* was particularly well-chosen. NDL was based at Bremen and the Deschimag AG Weser Shipyards, located in the same city, had built her. She was most prominent for her two very short funnels, which were so low that in 1932 they had to be raised to stop fallout from the fuel oil.

On her maiden voyage on June 16, 1929, the *Bremen* took the Blue Ribbon from the venerable *Mauretania,* which had retained it for over 20 years. The new liner thus took over from the *Kaiser Wilhelm der Grosse* and the *Deutschland,* whose performance at the beginning of the century had overturned the rules of the game, which gave the British pre-eminence on the legendary North Atlantic route. This record would later be beaten by the *Europa,* a similar ship which entered service the following year. This testimony

to Germany's renewal was due notably to the genius of the naval architects who equipped the vessel with a bulbous stem. This innovation facilitated a significant gain in speed by reducing drag. In 1932, the *Bremen* beat her own record of 28.14 knots after acquiring new turbines. The following year, however, she had to cede the Blue Ribbon to the *Rex,* which heralded the arrival of a new country in the race for speed on the North Atlantic.

On August 28, 1939, the *Bremen* arrived in the port of New York from where it was due to depart without passengers. Detained for two days by the American authorities, she set off for Murmansk, a port on the Kola penninsula. There she benefited from a benevolent neutrality in the context of the German-Soviet pact signed on August 23.

She came out of retirement on December 10 of the same year and reached Bremerhaven three days later, where she served as a floating barracks under camouflage until the Nazi authorities could decided on a

new role for her. They first thought of using her for the transport of troops for an invasion of Britain. When this plan was abandoned they considered the idea of converting her into an aircraft carrier. But Germany had no planes which could be based on a ship and the plan was forgotten.

So what became of this liner in the conflict? The German Admiralty would no doubt have found her a military task, but in March of 1941, a cabin boy took revenge after a bullying incident and sabotaged her. The ensuing fire caused the *Bremen* to sink and her hull was dismantled on the spot.

Length: 286 meters
(938 feet)
Width: 31.1 meters
(102 feet)
Tonnage: 51,656 meters
Cruising speed:
28.5 knots
Passengers: 2,200
Crew: 990 men

EXPRESS MAIL

The *Bremen* was one of the first ships to send postal deliveries using a sea plane, which was lauched from a catapult between the two funnels. This system had been adopted two years previously on the *Ile de France* and enabled precious hours to be saved at a period when civil aviation was still in its infancy. It could also have served important people who were in a hurry to arrive in America, but this facility was never exploited. This system of air relay had been tried out on the *Leviathan,* but by using a different procedure. Here, the airplane had been launched from a platform that extended from the rear of the liner.

PERILS OF THE SEA

Here was a ship whose civilian life, despite its success, was forever peppered with unexpected drama. Under different names, this liner suffered two fires in course of her completion-in in 1929 and during her conversion in 1949. Moreover, two workmen were killed in January of 1950, when a large piece of scaffolding on which they were working fell on them. On two occasions, under the Transat flag, she was driven against other ships in the port of Le Havre—in 1946 she drove against the hull of the *Paris* after the anchors broke, and in 1961 against a cargo ship in dock. Finally in December of 1957, an enormous wave caused so much damage that the *Liberté* was forced to return to Le Havre to undergo considerable repairs.

GERMANY, A CONVINCED EUROPEAN

The *Europa*, inaugurated in 1930, was the first of three liners that entered service during the Weimar Republic, and later in the German Federal Republic, to bear such a unifying name. In 1964, NDL gave this name to an eleven year-old liner belonging to the Svenska Amerika Linjen, then called the *Kungsholm*, which was traditionally ascribed to some of the Swedish company's ships. Sold to the Costa Armatori Group in 1981, she was damaged in a collision with the quay in the port of Cadiz, Spain. In late 1981, the Bremen shipyards completed the construction of a new *Europa*, a luxury liner commissioned by Hapag-Lloyd AG, the company that resulted from a merger between the two main shipping companies operating on the North Atlantic route.

I WRITE YOUR NAME, LIBERTY

The conversion of liners handed over by the vanquished is always loaded with a strong symbolic content. If Transat's custom had been followed, the *Europa* would have been given the name of a French province. La *Lorraine*, the name that was most often put forward, offered the advantage of perpetuating a tradition while at the same time drawing attention to the redrawn frontiers. It was Jules Moch, the vice-president of the Council, who opted for the very republican name, *Liberté*, and in doing so, sowed confusion into the minds of the Anglo Saxons. During the conflict, the American *Liberty ships* had sailed the seas provisioning five continents. French vindictiveness found expression in the names of the suites that referred to the main areas of action in the reconquest or to territories returned to France.

A Very Latin German

EUROPA
1930-1945
Lenght: 286.7 meters
(940 feet)
Width: 31.1 meters
(102 feet)
Tonnage: 49,746 tons
Speed: 28.5 knots
Passengers: 2,024
Crew: 970 men

LIBERTÉ
1950-1961
Length: 286.7 meters
(940 feet)
Width: 31.1 meters
(102 feet)
Tonnage: 51,839 tons
Passengers: 1,513
Crew: 990 men

There were some liners with such frustrated destinies that they never fulfilled the role to which they were assigned. The *Europa,* commissioned from Blohm and Voss in Hamburg, was one of these. NDL had planned to make her a quasi-sister to the *Bremen,* which was being built at the same time in a different shipyard. Similar to the latter, the *Europa* had a bulbous stem, but she was 70 centimeters longer and weighed 2,000 tons less. The idea was that both ships would be launched almost simultaneously and that they would pass each other in the middle of the Atlantic in their race for the Blue Riband. But on March 25, 1929, when she was close to completion, the *Europa* was the victim of a fire and the *Bremen* set out alone. When the *Europa* was finally ready, she set out on her maiden voyage from Bremerhaven on March 19, 1930, nearly a year later. The new arrival won the Blue Ri-

band before ceding to the *Bremen* once again. With the sucess of these two ships, NDL demonstrated a surprising commercial and financial recovery.

But the time of her splendour came to an end in 1939, when the Nazis gave the *Europa* a secondary role as a barracks in the port of Hamburg. She did not take part in any transportation of civilians or soldiers until May of 1945, when she finally conveyed troops. But by this time she was in the service of the Americans.

At the end of hostilities, the *Europa* was handed over to the French authorities. Under the name *Liberté,* she embarked on a new career on the occasion of which she encountered the ghost of one of her elder sisters. First she drove into the hull of the *Paris,* which had been blocking the port of Le Havre since April, 1939. Though she did not sink completely, due to the shallowness of the water, the repairs carried out on her were extensive. This work was done in the Saint Nazaire shipyards after she was refloated in April of the following year. But in

October, 1949, before her reconstruction was completed, she was again the victim of a fire. On August 17, 1959, she was ready to make her first crossing flying the French flag. In New York she received the warmest welcome of any liner since the *Normandie* in 1935. But she was not the same ship as before. Her power had fallen from 130,000 horsepower to 85,000. The reconfiguration and repair work had been so extensive that the liner now had competely different characterstics and fittings. But the ship was undoubtedly French; she boasted certain decorative elements that had been removed from the *Normandie* when she had been converted into a military vessel, and a menu that was worthy of the *French Line's* reputation.

She began a new life in tandem with the *Ile de France,* and also did occasional cruises. She carried the Transat colours high until the end of 1961, when she had to make room for the liner *France.* During her very full career, she carried more than a million passengers, including 400,000 after 1950.

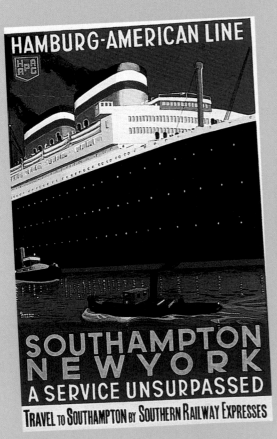

Red Star Line

ANVERS-LE CANADA

America this year by R.M.S. "Queen Mary"

Cunard White Star

LMS EXPRESS & CUNARD LINER

The HIGHEST STANDARD OF COMFORT IN RAIL AND OCEAN TRAVEL

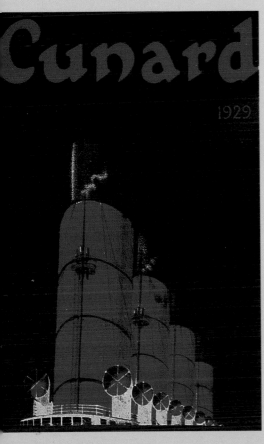

Cunard

1929

NACH NEW YORK

HAMBURG

HAPG

HAMBURG-AMERIKA LINIE

CUNARD LINE
USA & CANADA

A young man from Gascony

Entering service in 1931 and named in homage to a former director of Messageries Maritimes, the *Felix Roussel* was one of several ships in the "nautonaphte" series that were characterized by two very short square funnels.

Mixed liners of average dimensions, they were designed to travel at 16 knots, but this limited speed did not account for the many ports of call which punctuated the routes they served. These ships had the advantage of giant promenade decks in accomodation of the mild climates of the countries they visited. They were true sea omnibuses that embarked and disembarked passengers and freight at Port Said, Aden, Colombo, and Saigon, to name a few. A voyage from Marseilles to Japan or Australia took around one and a half months, and had little in common with performance on the North Atlantic routes. At the beginning of the century, the concern for speed dictated the amount of coal required for the crossing. By contrast, the ships that provided links with Africa or Asia had opportunities to take on coal at their different ports of call.

Though certainly not giants of the sea, these liners offered wealthy passengers some very luxurious surroundings. The décor on the *Felix Roussel* was strongly influenced by Khmer art, which could be found in the salons, the dining room or the music room. But other sources of inspiration coalesced on board as well. For example, the first class swimming pool was typical Art Deco, while the *Georges Philippar* had more classic décor in the style of the castles on the Loire, with suites that represented the history of French furniture. The *Aramis,* however, was an evocation of Crete.

Providing a large number of places in emigrant class for soldiers on leave and French people from Indo-China, the *Felix Roussel* operated on the route to China and Japan until 1940. The French armistice then took her by surprise at Port Said where she was requisitioned by the British Admiralty. Put onto troop transports, she distinguished herself most notably in the evacuation of women and children from Singapore, following the seizure of the city in 1942.

Returning to civilian life in 1946, the *Felix Roussel* underwent an overhaul at Dunkirk until 1948, during which she lost her two ungraceful funnels and gained a single one that was oval and taller. She went back into service on the Far Eastern route before being sold in 1955 to the Swiss company, Arosa. This came as a result of a fall in passenger traffic due to the independence of the countries of Indo-China. Renamed the *Arosa Sun,* she was put on the North Atlantic route from Bremerhaven, serving New York and Quebec. She went back to the black hull she had sported at the start of her career, which had been painted white after the overhaul in 1946. In 1959, after the failure of Arosa, she served as a floating hotel for the workmen of a Dutch company until her demolition in 1974.

Length: 171.25 meters (562 feet)
Width: 20.8 meters (68 feet)
Tonnage: 16,774 tons
Speed: 16 knots
Passengers: 1898
Crew: 258 men

THE SPIRIT OF A PRESIDENT

Georges Philippar, the president of Messageries Maritimes, left behind a reputation in merchant shipping for the originality of his views. A resolute supporter of innovation rather than imitation, he was also a forward-looking spirit. He invented the word "nautonaphte," in describing a long series of diesel powered liners, to avoid the use of "motor ships," which was "too English" in his eyes. Originally from Gers and a great fan of Alexandre Dumas, he saw to it that on each liner the decoration of at least one area made reference to his hero. The names of the musketeers were also given to four of his ships.

THE MYSTERY OF THE *GEORGES PHILIPPAR*

The *Felix Roussel's* sister ship, the *Georges Philippar*, sank while returning from her maiden voyage to Yokohama, which had begun on February 26, 1932. When the liner left Marseilles, there was a rumour circulating that arms for Japan, then at war with China, were being stored in the hold. A short time later, the ship's radio received a message that a there was a bomb aboard, at Port Said, a search uncovered explosives. On April 1, the liner reached the Shanghai river. The journalist Albert Londres embarked on her to return to France. During the night of May 15-16, when the ship was en route for Djibouti, it was ravaged by fire. Of the 815 passengers, around sixty died. It is thought that the fire was caused by an electrical fault. However, Albert Londres' death in the fire continued to fuel rumours. The journalist had mentioned that he was in possession of a report on Bolshevik involvement in the events that were rocking China. His notes were never found. The two friends he met on board, who were the only people to hear his secrets, were among the survivors, but they were killed near Rome when the plane that was taking them to France crashed.

THE *ARAMIS*

The *Felix Roussel's* other sister ship was put on the Far East route in 1932. During the Second World War, she was converted into an auxiliary battle cruiser, fitted with eight 136 guns and sent off to Saigon in 1939. On April 11, 1942, she was requisitioned by the Japanses authorities, sailing under her flag of origin and Japanese command until June 2, 1942, when the French crew were dismissed. With the *Gripsholm*, she took part in the repatriation of Japanese and American diplomats to their countries of origin. She was sunk on August 18, 1944, by an American sumarine near the Philippines.

77

WITNESSES OF A SORRY DEPARTURE

The speed of the new Italian liner made it the subject of such hype that some VIPs made reservations on the maiden voyage in order to be present at the breaking of a record. But as a result of thefts at the start of the crossing, some of them opted to embark on a rival ship. Among the passengers on that maiden voyage were Harold Vanderbilt and Jimmy Walter, a former mayor of New York, and one Francis Spellman, who was taking up his new post as Bishop of Boston, and who would later resurface at the marriage of Grace Kelly and Prince Rainier of Monaco.

THE HALES TROPHY

From the middle of the 19th century, the Blue Riband was an imaginary, unofficial trophy, that sometimes came to embody a banner whose length in meters corresponded to the number of knots attained by the fastest liner. In 1935, Harold Hales, a British MP, presented the *Rex* with a trophy in recognition for her being the fastest. It was agreed that this trophy would be passed from ship to ship, but that a ship whose record was beaten would retain it for three months in order to have a chance to win it back. This explains why the *Rex* still claimed it when the *Normandie's* performance had already deprived her of it. This trophy of extremely dubious taste combined references to Greek mythology, a colored globe, a portrait of the donor, and pictures of various liners, including the *Great Western*. Cunard, which claimed they did not wish to compete for speed, refused it. It is now on display in New York's South Street Seaport Museum.

Below: The Rex was the inspiration for Fellini's film Amarcord.

Length: 268.20 meters
Width: 29.50 meters
Tonnage : 51,062 tons
Cruising speed: 29 knots
Passagers : 2,308
Crew: 756 men

A King Struck Down

On January 2, 1932, at Mussolini's instigation, the Compagnie Italia was established, as result of a merger between Cosulich, Lloyd Sabaudo and Navigazione Generale Italinana. Earlier, the latter had received government subsidies for the construction of a larger and faster liner than the *Roma* and the *Augustus*. The government's chief ambition was to demonstrate Italy's capacity to compete for speed with the main transatlantic companies, and to gain the Blue Riband.

Launched in August of 1931, the *Rex* began her maiden voyage from Genoa on September 27, 1932, exactly ten years after Mussolini's seizure of power. For Constanzo Ciano, the transport minister, this was a fine opportunity to celebrate the liners which would defend "the discipline, technical prowess and spirit of enterprise of the new Italy". But the *Rex*, a true instrument of propaganda, did not set out on her maiden voyage to satisfy Il Duce, who prized precision above all else. In reality, she was not ready to go to sea, and a problem with the turbo generator

immobilised her for several days at Gibraltar.

Her spoiled start represented only a mere hitch in the Fascists' plans, and in August, 1933, the *Rex* took the Blue Riband from the *Bremen*. The same year, she improved on her record, attaining 28.92 knots. Her captain was the first to be seen accepting the sculptured representation of victory, the Hales Trophy.

The Admiral's Service

The flagship of the Italian fleet, the *Rex* focused her publicity on the fact that to reach New York she took a more southerly route than her British, French or German rivals. The crossings took place in more clement conditions, following a less dangerous route. The atmosphere on board was completely typical of the Italian liners, which raised idleness to a real art of living at sea. This was especially noticeable on the *Rex* which introduced the concept of the lido-deck with three open-air swimming pools, parasols and even the use of sand. The decoration was partly modern and partly inspired by 18th-century Italian design.

Italy's entry into the war forced the

Rex into a period of confinement in the Mediterranean. She did not take part in the conflict, however; the military authorities merely camouflaged her under netting. The ship was first moored at Bari and then moved to Trieste. The armistice signed with the Allies in September, 1943, did not affect her inactivity, since Italy immediately declared war on Germany, which continued to occupy her terrain. Seeing the displacement of the liner as a means of blocking the port of Triest, Allied airplanes bombarded the vessel on September 8, 1944. The *Rex* sank, destroyed by rockets. After the end of the Second World War, there were plans to lift her, but it was found that she had been pillaged and her restoration would be too costly. She was dismantled on site in an operation that took more than ten years.

Length 238.3 meters
(782 feet)
Width: 29.3 meters (96 feet)
Tonnage: 48,502 tons
Speed: 29.3 knots
Passengers: 2,200
Crew: 786 men.

Between Tradition and New Regime

Lloyd Sabaudo, one of the principal Italian shipping companies, was owned mainly by the royal family. Within the context of redeploying the national fleet, the Fascist regime offered the firm a subsidy to construct a prestigious new liner, as it had done earlier with the Navigazione Generale Italiana, which had led to the launch of the *Rex.* The ship was entrusted to the Adriatico Shipyards near to Trieste.

The *Conte di Savoia,* which set out on her maiden voyage from Genoa on November 30, 1932, was of a very characteristic design. She respected the tradition by which Lloyd Sabaudo liners bore the title and name of a member of the royal family, but it also satisfied Mussolini's wish to strengthen the prestige of Italian shipping industry and the nation. Though not a sister ship—she was ordered by a different company from a different shipyard—she was first mate to the *Rex,* with whom she carried high the colors of the regime. She was, to some extent,

the *Rex's* double by reason of the similarities in her design and career. Like the *Rex,* she was distinguished by the inclusion of a lido deck and the adoption of a decoration which harked back to a glorious past, most notably a marble function room replicating the Palazzo Colonna in Rome and an Etruscan-style swimming pool, also surrounded by sand. As well, she experienced problems on her maiden voyage. As she was approaching the American coast, a safety valve burst. The tons of water that rushed in put out the ship's dynamo and the liner was without electricity for several hours. A sailor roped himself and climbed down the hull to plug the hole. His name, Gennaro Amatruda, and the 800 or so dollars the passengers collected for him as a reward have earned their place in history.

Like the *Rex,* the *Conte di Savoia* served the Naples-Genoa-New York route, also calling at a French Mediterranean port, first Villefranche sur Mer and later Cannes, which the di-

rectors of the company felt offered better security arrangements for important ships dropping anchor there.

She surpassed the *Rex* in one respect: she was one of the first superliners to be fitted with gyroscopic stabilizers. Three in number, they used new anti-roll technology. The innovation was such that the company concentrated all its publicity on the additional comfort it offered passengers.

The merchant career of the *Conte di Savoia* lasted a very short time. Laid up for a while in 1939, she then undertook some round trips and was inactive after 1940. In September, 1943, she was sunk in shallow water near Venice by the Americans. Although her hull was raised, she was never used again.

Left: The Conte di Savoia *on one of her rare cruises to Egypt. The liner's funnels, like those of the* Rex, *are unusual in that they have ventilation valves. Here they are shown open.*
Right: The Conte di Savoia *in the port of Genoa. Next to her is a liner belonging to the Dollar Line, recognizable by the sign on its funnel.*

VIEW OF THE DECK

Originally a holdover from sailing ships, the decks were progressively fitted out to become an area for social activities. This transformation was achieved most notably by the protection of certain areas by windows, which made it possible to use the decks under overcast skies on the Atlantic. The reduction in the number of funnels on liners, which started after the First World War, also made it possible to have on the top deck a large area available to passengers. In particular, passengers could lie side by side on the transatlantic liners, protected by blankets, with an army of waiters waiting to satisfy their smallest desires. Deck games were a very old idea, having been installed on the *Great Eastern* in 1860. Often demanding high levels of skill, these games were further complicated by the movement of the sea. One of the oldest games was undoubtedly quoits. Its consisted of an oval painted on the ground and divided into numbered squares, each denoting a number of points. One had to land a quoit (a flat piece of wood) on one of these squares by pushing it with a stick. Passengers could also indulge in croquet, tennis, shooting, hoops and volleyball. The swimming pools were open air when the sea route went through a sufficiently mild climate.

Our animal friends

The decks also served the comfort of other customers that needed pampering: dogs. Even at the time of the *Titanic,* it was fashionable to take one's pet on trips. This was how, during the famous sinking of the *Titanic,* a first class passenger named Henry Sleeper managed to put his Pekinese, Sun Yat Sen, on a life boat.

Traditionally, walking the dogs was done by the crew's butcher. Later a team of grooms were given this responsibility. Over time, the beloved pups became even more spoiled. On the *Normandie* they had the advantage of kennels in one of the funnels. When Transat brought this liner into service they gave the dogs' owners a special menu for their companions, which was almost as varied as their own.

The game of quoits, one of the oldest pastimes practised on board liners and one of the most popular.

Despite the rolling of the ship, the style is confident and the strike is close.

82

A promotional
picture of
a tennis match
on the Atlantic.

All the Fairies in a Cradle

She was the finest, the most elegant, the most refined of craft and took the ocean-liner style to its zenith. She was also the fastest, seizing the Blue Riband from the *Rex* on her maiden voyage, the first time a French ship had done so. She took the trophy again two years later, after conceding it to the *Queen Mary,* one year her junior, which retained it without a break from 1938 to 1952.

Transat's directors felt that speed would bring in the profits. They needed a liner capable of doing the transatlantic crossing in four days and a few hours, and perhaps even two sufficiently fast liners to run a weekly crossing in each direction. For the owners, such a time gain would mean a substantial reduction in running costs, which was necessary in the very sluggish international environment. The high fuel consumption caused by the 30 knot crossing and her 160,000 horsepower would be compensated by a larger number of passengers.

The launch took place on October 29, 1932, at the Penhoët Shipyard at Saint Nazaire, in the presence of Madame Lebrun, the wife of the French President, who had named the liner. For this event it had been necessary to deepen the fairway.

The hull of the *Normandie* was designed by Vlakimir Yourkevitch, a Russian émigré who had participated in the construction of Czar Nicholas II's war fleet. Compared with other ships of the time, she had a special shape intended to reduce water resistance—a streamlined stem of a pronounced concave shape, rounded, like that of the *Bremen*.

After a delay caused by the economic slump of the period, the liner entered service on May 29, 1935, at Le Havre, following three days of festivities and a gala evening attended by the French president.

For the *Normandie,* Le Havre was equipped with a new maritime railroad station next to the quay. The port of New York also needed to build a new quay to accommodate this 313.75 meter giant, the longest liner ever built until the *France.* The Archbishop of Paris and the Bishop of Rouen quarrelled as to who should have the privilege of naming her. A whole nation had provided its best artefacts and demonstrated the best of its *savoir-faire* for her. The building of the *Normandie,* for which Transat had obtained the largest subsidy ever offered, required the country's best engineers and its greatest interior designers. In return, she gave the French something to be proud of. As had happened with the *Queen Mary,* tens of thousands of jobs had been created.

The *Normandie* was given the purest design possible. She had elegant lines obtained most notably by a stem reminiscent of the clippers, a rounded overhang from the prow, eleven decks that rose up like an amphitheatre and very restrained superstructures allowing for the largest maximum passenger area on deck.

Length: 313,75 meters (1030 feet)
Width: 35.9 meters (118 feet)
Tonnage: 79,280 tons
Speed: 30 knots
Passengers: 1,972
Crew: 1,355 men

Right: As she leaves dry dock in the port of Le Havre, the Normandie passes the Ile de France.

THE TRIUMPH OF THE *NORMANDIE*

The maiden voyage of the *Normandie* was a veritable triumph, as much during her days in port at Le Havre as during her crossing, which was completed in four days, three hours and 15 minutes.

Her progress up the Hudson in full regalia took place in the presence of an enthusiastic crowd. The *Normandie* became the liner on which one had to cross the Atlantic, the holder of the Blue Riband, which offered a window onto French taste. For the first

crossing a crowd of writers was on board either as press correspondants or invitees. Colette, Blaise Cendrars, Philippe Soupault, Claude Farrere, all recorded their invaluable impressions of the voyage. In 1935, Cassandre signed a poster for the *Normandie*, an updated version of which indicated: "On January 1, 1939, 60 round trips, 115,000 passengers". On August 23, 1939, the *Normandie* set out from the Havre for her 137th crossing, which was also to be her last.

THE *NORMANDIE'S* PROPELLERS

The shape of the stem was such that drag was reduced to a minimum, and with very little backwash. The only problem was the strong vibrations at the rear. These were suppressed after modifications to the four propellers in May, 1936, after six months in dry dock. The choice of four-bladed rather than three-bladed propellers enabled the *Normandie* to retake the Blue Riband from the *Queen Mary* in 1937. The liner would have its propellers mentioned on yet another occasion when in September of the same year she made almost the entire crossing on three propellers, having lost the fourth at sea.

85

The *Normandie:* the art of living

The *Normandie's* decoration was truly a floating extension of the Exhibition of Decorative Arts, which took place in Paris in 1925. It called upon a multiplicity of artists and designers, most notably for the first class cabins, which were each treated in a different manner.

The aesthetic success of the public spaces was explained by a technical decision that the Germans had planned for the *Vaterland* but later abandoned, in regard to discharge of smoke from the engines.

Traditionally, the funnels occupied a large volume of depth; by contrast, the *Normandie's* architects chose to separate the smoke conduits and push them against the sides of the ship. This meant that they only joined up at the level of the envelope of the funnel in its visible part. By freeing the space above the two funnels, it was possible to create unbroken vistas with no supporting columns in the way.

Perspectives

It was this absence of breaks that explained the impression of space on the decks of the *Normandie;* it also allowed the creation of a series of rooms of magnificent size. It was in the first class areas that this was best illustrated.

The architects Patou and Pacon worked on "C" deck, where the large first class dining room was one of the centers for social life. Extending 1,000 meters (3,300 feet) in length and 8 meters (26 feet) high, it was the largest room ever built on a ship. The hall, which could accommodate 150 tables, was designed to feed all the first class passengers at one sitting. The ceiling was all in one piece and decorated with gilded caissons, and a rubber carpet on the floor took up the ship's motifs in black, navy blue and light blue.

This dining room did not take up the complete width of the liner, and its reinforced walls avoided the need for supports. As a result of this configuration, the room had no windows. She was lit by two giant chandeliers and 38 wall lights, designed by Lalique. The lack of natural ventilation necessitated air conditioning, the first to be installed on a liner.

At center of the dining hall was a statue entitled "Pax" by Dejean; on the walls there were pieces of engraved and carved glass; and at each end six meter (20 foot) high base reliefs. Complemented by a smaller room—designated the banqueting suite—the dining hall was shut off by a monumental door adorned with medallions representing towns in Normandy. Behind this was a large hall, at the end of which an enamel paneled partition hid a chapel for Catholic and Protestant services. In 1936, this was adapted for use as a synagogue.

The option taken for the dining room at this level was not to give it windows, which had the advantage of exploiting the lighting to the maximum and also of gaining space in which more outer cabins overlooking the sea could be located. The *Normandie* had more of these than most other large liners.

Right: First class cabin.
Below: The large first class dining room designed by Patout and Pacon. In the extension of this, beyond the great hall, was the chapel.

86

PIERRE PATOUT'S LINERS

Before taking charge of the fitting out of the *Normandie* in 1934, Pierre Patout worked with the cabinet maker Jacques Ruhlmann on the decoration of the *Atlantique*, a superb liner serving the South American route which caught fire in January, 1933, less than 18 months after entering service. (A third liner was also built to Pierre Patout's designs.) When he became a land architect once more, he designed a building to fit on a parcel of land 90 meters (300 feet) long and 2.4 meters (8 feet) and 10 meters (33 feet) wide, between the railroad and the Boulevard Victor in Paris. The apartment block was clearly inspired by the shape of the liners, as seen from the grande epoque with tiered terraces on the "prow," just like the decks on the *Normandie*. Patout reserved an apartment for himself at the pointed end of the "stem," facing the west. On Transat's flagship, the captain's apartment was also located at the extremity of the sun deck, designed by Marjorelle and Remon.

ON "A" DECK

The view from the top deck, designed by Expert and Bouwens de Boijen, offered the same feeling of immensity. The theatre, the first on a liner, looked onto the upper hall which linked the large first class lounge with a dance floor, the smoking room decorated with sculptured panels painted gold, and the grand staircase which led to the grill room. A vista of around 170 meters stretched out before the passengers' eyes.

Above: The great hall and in the background the stairs leading to the chapel. Left: The famous Captain Villarm, photographed on the Ile de France. He was also an officer on the Normandie.

Prematurely aged

For a seaman, whether merchant or military, the end of a ship is always difficult. But on the whole, he finds a glorious death (destruction by fire or in an accident) is more normal and much worthier than annihilation in a breaker's yard.

General de Gaulle considered old age to be like a shipwreck. The *Normandie's* deterioration, which began after only four years of activity, was a slow agony that lasted eight years. No other liner had suffered such a cruel and unworthy fate. It all began when inactivity was forced upon her from August 28, 1939, when the start of the Second World War caught the *Normandie* unaware in New York, just like the *Queen Mary,* which was soon joined by the hastily completed *Queen Elizabeth.* While the two Queens were to see active service in the conflict, however, the French Government preferred that the *Normandie* remain in the United States as a safety measure. But the debacle of 1940 and the new political situation in France aroused the mistrust of the Americans, who suspected the *Normandie's* crew of sabotage. So on May 15, 1941, members of the coastguard began occupying the ship.

Naturalization

The Japanese attack on Pearl Harbour on December 7, 1941 brought the United States into the conflict. Five days later, the *Normandie* was requisitioned. An effort was made to remove all the ship's fittings in hopes of converting her into a troop ship. On January 1, 1942, while the refit continued, the liner was officially renamed the *Lafayette.*

On February 9, 1942, around 2:30 pm, an accident occurred as a workman was using a blowlamp to remove the lighting columns from the immense dining room. Some life belts made of kapok, a very inflammable material, were being stored close by. One spark from the blowlamp was enough to set fire to them, igniting a fire which could not be put out quickly enough. There was general panic, and the

New York firemen, who were alerted ten minutes after the outbreak of fire, evacuated the 3,000 workmen on board. In the confusion, a member of the coastguard was killed, along with 128 other casualties.

Wait, wait ...

The fire was put out in four hours, but the ship was weighed down by the 6,000 tons of water that had accumulated in the upper part, causing the *Normandie* to list dangerously to port. Despite measures to remove the water, the ship continued to list and got worse as the tide came in, attaining an angle of 35% by midnight; half an hour later the hull was abandoned. The ship capsized at 0230 hours. There was a wait of more than a year and a half until what was left of the *Normandie* was

refloated in October, 1943. For this delicate and onerous operation, her superstructures were taken down.

In her sinister state of destitution, the ship was towed up the Hudson to a drydock in November. Experts decided that her rehabilitation would cost too much, so in 1946, the Navy sold the hull to a demolition contractor for $161,000.

USELESS SAFETY MEASURES

It was ironic that the *Normandie* should perish in a fire when she had been equipped with so many fire-combatting devices; the ship had more than 1,000 fire detectors and 224 manual fire alarms. Unfortunately, most of this equipment had been taken out during the conversion of the *Normandie* into a troop ship. And although the Americans had hired on a fire brigade, they had not worked out a plan of attack with any of the crew remaining aboard when the ship had its own naval fire corps. In the end, it seems that the New York firemen ignored the advice of the French crew, who were far more familiar with the ship. In any case, the *Normandie* could have been saved if the fire had been left to develop without hindrance. It was the poorly managed human intervention which was the cause of her demise.

HIGH PLACES

For a very long time, the area for first class passengers was concentrated on several decks in the center of the liner, where the rolling and pitching were less noticeable. In 1962, however, the *France* organized the different classes of passenger on a longitudinal plan. This organization on several decks explains the importance of the grand double staircase, which first appeared on the *Borgogne* in 1886. Gradually, all liners boasted a grand staircase where belles appeared on the arm of gentlemen in evening dress. Apart from the grand lounge, liners also had a number of public spaces, which, at the beginning of the century, resulted in the segregation of the sexes. The smoking room was for men, while one lounge was reserved for women. It was only later that integration became the rule. The shopping arcade was also an essential part of a liner's social

DEAD MAN OVERBOARD

For the service personnel on ships, initiatives were permitted so long as they were sensible ones. But what zeal motivated the lad cleaning the cabin of a first class passenger to throw into the sea the ash from the ash trays and also from a container?

The furious lady-passenger went right to the captain to complain that her husband had been thrown overboard. She could not be separated from the urn containing the cremated remains of her dead husband.

scene. Located at the same level as the embarkation hall, of which it was an extension, the shopping arcade reached its zenith in the thirties. One of the most successful arcades was that of the *Atlantique*, a superb liner on which Pierre Patout

had worked before becoming one of the architects of the *Normandie*. Lined with deluxe shops, this 137 meter (450 foot) long 6 meter (20 foot) high mall had an elegance worthy of the finest streets in Paris.

There was even a car showroom for the first time ever.

Above: The ladies' salon on the German liner, Columbia *(at the end of 19th century) Above: The mixed first class salon on the* France *in 1912.*

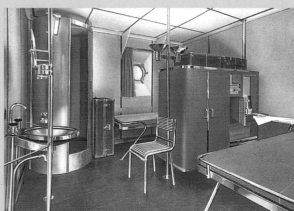

Above: The celebrated shopping mall on the Atlantique, which entered service in 1931 and whose career ended as a result of a fire on January 5, 1933.

Above: First class cabin on the France in 1962.

Left: First class passengers on the Champlain.

THE QUEEN'S NAME

Originally, the new British liner was to be called the *Victoria*. Due to a misunderstanding, though, she ended up with the name of King George V's wife (Mary) rather than that of his mother (Victoria). To christen a ship *Victoria*, the king's consent was needed, but the company's request was ambiguous: would His Majesty permit them to give the liner the name of the most remarkable and illustrious queen of England? George V took the request as a very great compliment to himself and his wife, and immediately gave his consent.

Actually, the name Queen Mary proved to be a fortunate choice in the period which immediately followed, with the merger of the two largest British companies on the North Atlantic route, whose ships were differentiated by the names of their vessels. The names of the Cunard liners traditionally ended in "ia," and White Star liners in "ic." The name "Queen Mary" offended nobody's sensibilities.

Length: 310.5 meters
(297 feet)
Width: 36 meters
(118 feet)
Tonnage: 80,774 tons
Speed : 32 knots
Passengers:
approx 2,190
Crew: 1,101 men

An iron fist in a velvet glove

The *Queen Mary* reflects perfectly the different epochs she has been through during the course of her long career, which is not yet over.

At the end of the twenties, the Cunard Line realized it needed to renew its aging fleet on the North Atlantic route, which was being served by ships designed before the Great War—the *Mauretania* and the *Aquitania,* both with impeccable service records, and the *Berengaria* from the German fleet. The entry into service of the *Bremen* and the *Europa* in 1929 and 1930, respectively, confirmed the danger presented by a new foreign fleet, of which the *Ile de France* in 1927 had already shown its powers of attraction.

The Velvet

Work started on the new vessel at the end of 1930, just before the economic crisis hit Europe. As a result of financial difficulties, construction had to be halted when the hull was still unfinished. The stoppage put 13,000 out of work. The severity of the recession prompted the British Government in 1934 to advance a loan of ú10 million sterling, in return for a merger between Cunard and White Star, the two principal British shipping companies, which

had both found themselves in financial difficulties. On September 26 of the same year, the liner was launched in the presence of George V and his wife, Queen Mary, whose name she bore.

She made her first crossing from Southampton in May 27, 1936, after running aground. With a speed of 30.63 knots, she quickly regained the Blue Riband from the *Normandie,* which had won it the previous year. The Transat liner, the only French ship to win the Riband, regained it the following year. A year later, in 1938, the *Queen Mary* beat her own record with 31.69 knots. It was not until 1952 that another liner, the *United States,* would take it from her with a speed of 35.59 knots.

The *Queen Mary* had her share of teething troubles as well. She lacked stability, her funnels emitted too much soot over the decks and her propellers were not efficient enough. She had to undergo a substantial overhaul after being put into service, during which the grand salon had to be reconfigured to reinforce the hull. Later, her stabilizers needed to be modified. Nevertheless, the *Queen Mary* became the flagship of the British merchant

navy by means of her luxury, which many considered to be the equal of her French rival, the *Normandie.*

After returning to civilian life in 1946, she pursued a glorious, twenty-year transatlantic career on the same route, but this time in tandem with the *Queen Elizabeth.* This stage of her career only came to an end just before the entry into service of the *Queen Elizabeth II,* which was better suited to the new economic conditions.

.... And the Iron

If the *Queen Mary* persists in the memory, it is as much for flying the flag of the monarchy high in peace time as for her service during the Second World War. The semi-retirement she currently enjoys confers on her a special status, since she is one of the few ships—apart from the *Great Britain,* built in the 19th century—to have a career in harbor.

93

The Queen Mary leaving the shipyards on the Clyde at Glasgow.

A Queen at War

During the Second World War, the contribution of the British sovereigns was exemplary. King George VI, at Winston Churchill's side, helped to restore the morale of a sorely tested public, and the Queen refused to go into exile with her children right until the end of hostilities. Can a name be more prophetic? The two Queens, the *Queen Mary* at the head, took part valiantly in a conflict which would last more than five years. The liner transported up to 6,000 soldiers on one crossing unescorted, her speed being her principal defence.

The outbreak of hostilities took the *Queen Mary* by surprise in the port of New York, where she arrived on September 3, 1939. But her period of inactivity lasted only six months, and she quickly became the first British liner to participate in the conflict. After being dressed in a grey uniform and equipped with cannons, she left America on March 21, 1940, and reached Sydney, Australia on April 17. It was in Australia, which was still unaffected by the turbulence of war, that she was adapted in record time to be a troop ship. On May 5, 1940, she assumed her new role and was ready to transport 5,500 men. She began by taking Australian soldiers to Great Britain.

The rest of her military career followed the events which marked different stages in the conflict. Once the risk of a German invasion of England was over, she began a period in southerly and tropical climes, for which her service on the Atlantic had not prepared her, insofar that her installations were not designed for warm climates. Despite this handicap, she transported Australians to North Africa, but not through the Suez Canal because of her size.

After the Japanese attack on Pearl Harbour, the center of the conflict moved to the South Pacific. The *Queen Mary* was therefore used to transport American soldiers to Australia. She then returned to the North Atlantic route and conveyed American and Canadian troops to Scotland. Her return journeys were devoted to the transport of European soldiers and prisoners of war to plantations in Canada and in the southern United States.

As one might imagine, such activity was not undertaken without peril. Though she managed to thwart an attack by a German submarine in March, 1942, she did cause the loss of the British cruiser, *Curacao*. As a result of poor zig-zag synchronization to protect them both from attacks, the *Queen Mary* she cut this military vessel in two, causing the deaths of 338 sailors.

In 1946, the *Queen Mary* returned to civilian life, covered with glory for her role in the conflict and after taking war brides to America. In a way, this ensured her lineage, since her exemplary service during the war prompted the construction of the *United States,* which entered service in 1952 and took the Blue Riband from her.

A MODEL BATH

Churchill, the principal architect of the victory who paid dearly for it in the 1945 elections, had a knowledge of naval matters that were deeply anchored in his upbringing. Appointed First Lord of the Admiralty in 1911, he had taken in the Great War. During the following global conflict, he made three crossings on the *Queen Mary.* It is said that that once, in a bath filled with water in the presence of a general and an admiral, he used model ships to simulate the landing operations in the artificial ports installed off *Normandy,* to convince himself of the feasibility of the project. The war was won in a bathroom behind closed doors.

THE QUEEN MOTHER

After the war, the *Queen Mary* returned to service with an aura of enormous popularity. However, the competition from the air was making itself known, and the company found that its profits were turing into operational losses. So on August 18, 1967, the liner was bought by the city of Long Beach, California. Her last crossing from Southampton at the end of that year lasted more than two months. It was her 1,001st. She took to the seas for two cruises before berthing permanently in California, near Los Angeles. In 31 years, in commercial and military service, she had transported more than two million passengers and sailed the equivalent of 153 times around the world.

Since 1971, she has been fitted out as a floating hotel, a maritime museum and a conference center. As American giganticism is never far away, she has been joined by the *Spruce Goose*, a real monster of American aviation. This sea plane, 92 meters long and built by Howard Hughes, made only one flight of 1,000 meters in 1947.
So what is the Queen Mary's future? After gaining great popularity immediately after her conversion, she now earns only a modest income. Her fate depends on the revenue her owners can expect from her. It is as if she is still sailing the seas.

Above: The Queen Mary anchored at Long Beach, California, with her engines removed.

THE DUTCH IN THE NEW WORLD

In 1609, Henry Hudson reconnoitred a river which he went up as far as the present city of Albany. Although he was English, Hudson explored this new land in the name of the Dutch East India Company, for which he thought he had discovered a new passage to the East Indies. Four years later, Adriaen Block established the first colony in the region, called New Holland.

In 1626, the governor of this region bought Manhattan Island from the Iroquois and named the colony he had founded New Amsterdam. The city remained Dutch until 1664, when it was surrender to the British without resistance. The place names still preserve many reminders of the Dutch presence; the Bronx owes its name to Jonas Bronck who acquired the territoryin 1639, and Brooklyn is a distortion of Breukelen, a locality near Utrecht.

LOVE SETTLEMENT

The *Nieuw Amsterdam* deserves its name, meaning "Dutch Love". In 1967, her owners planned to lay up the ship and send her for demolition. This prospect aroused such an outcry of public opinion, however, that the directors of the Holland Amerika Lijn recanted and decided to proceed with the necessary repairs for the continuance of her career. Thanks to the man in the street, the liner enjoyed an extended life until she was laid up in December, 1973, and finally sold for scrap in January, 1974.

Length: 231.2 meters
(758 feet)
Width: 26.8 meters
(88 feet)
Tonnage: 36,387 tons
Cruising speed:
22.8 knots
Passengers: 1,220
Crew: 695 men

The Conquest of New York

The Dutch shipping companies had always focused their efforts on the routes linking the Netherlands with its colonies, particularly the East Indies. However, once the repercussions of the world slump were over, the Dutch began building a liner in Rotterdam for service on the North Atlantic route. Though the decision was prompted by the increase in passenger traffic on the New York route, was also helped by the economic situation in the Netherlands. The shipyards were experiencing a serious recession and the construction of a large new liner (of more than 36,000 tons) would provide work for a large number of underemployed workers. It was this situation that justified state aid to the Holland Amerika Lijn.

The name of the new ship, which set out on its inaugural crossing on May 10, 1938, figured symbolically in the collective imagination of the Dutch, since they were the people who founded New York.

The decoration of the *Nieuw Amsterdam* referred proudly to this glorious past. On the liner, there was a portrait of Peter Stuyvesant, the last Dutch governor of the city, and also a superb model of a ship of that era.

The Military Parenthesis

Like most of the other large liners, the *Nieuw Amsterdam* participated in the Second World War, but she was used by the British Admiralty. Her military career began in 1940, after the German invasion of Holland, which caused her to remain in New York at the end of a cruise. The British converted her into a troopship at Halifax, Nova Scotia. Under the Cunard flag, she then transported more than 370,000 soldiers to

Asia and the Pacific. Her service record was so exceptional that she received an enthusiastic welcome on her return to Rotterdam on April 26, 1946, when peace returned.

A Perfect Civilian Career

The *Nieuw Amsterdam,* which found immediate public favor even before the war, was one of the most popular liners for transatlantic crossings.

She retained her popularity after the end of hostilities. From October 29, 1947, she again sailed the New York route. In 1961, she adopted the light grey color which characterized liners from the Netherlands, and she was nicknamed the "Peace Ship".

She also underwent a successful "open heart" operation: in August, 1967, her boilers were showing serious signs of weakness, so the starboard side of the hull was cut for the installation of replacement boilers, which were taken from an old American battle cruiser.

NIEUW AMSTERDAM

THE POST-WAR PERIOD:1945

Once more, the fleets were ruined and the ports blocked with wrecks. Once more, ships changed their nationality, while those designed before or during the conflict took their final shape. Everything was ready to start up again as before. But things had changed. The colonial empires were coming to an end, and countries which had gained independence were holding their heads high. The new geopolitical reality led to the closure of some very long-established routes – to the Far East and Algeria, for example. The drying up of immigration to South America or Australia also confirmed the decline of long distance liners.

On the North Atlantic route, for which so many giants had been built, a requiem mass was said at the end of the fifties. By 1957, air travellers equalled sea passengers in number. Later, airliners would rapidly and inexorably reduce the ocean liners' share of the market to almost nothing. So what remains of these great crossings?
The liners which had been designed for cruise work did not incur financial losses for their owners. As well, The *Queen Elizabeth II* was a witness to the new age, but she was also an actor in the new developments.

A Very Civil Soldier

The *Queen Elizabeth's* career began in an unorthodox manner, for although she designed to alternate with the *Queen Mary* on the North Atlantic route, she first embarked on a military life, for which we was hastily camouflaged in grey paint. Launched on September 27, 1938, from the shipyards of the River Clyde in Scotland, the *Queen Elizabeth* was named by the present Queen Mother. She was scheduled to enter service in March, 1940. When war was declared in September, 1939, the construction of the world's largest and finest liner was incomplete. To free the drydock for military vessels, the ship was completed hastily.

She docked at New York on March 7, 1940. In November, she was en route to Singapore as a troopship. In the spring of 1941, she had a similar role to the *Queen Mary,* conveying Australian troops to North Africa. The *Queen Elizabeth's* service record merged with the *Queen Mary's,* and her movements continued to change as the conflict evolved. She even broke the world record for the number of passengers transported on a single voyage, with around 6,000 soldiers on board.

The *Queen Elizabeth* was the first liner to return to civilian life. She arrived in Southampton on March 6, 1946, to be fitted out with a normal configuration after six years' military service. Her lines recalled those of the *Normandie,* which had inspired her engineers. One testimony to this was the open shape of her decks. She was capable of accommodating on 2,273 passengers,

with more than a third in third class. The war had led to a democratization of sea travel, which meant the appearance of a new middle class clientele, consisting of veterans from two world wars. As a result, first class cabins were so much in demand that reservations had to made a year in advance.

The civilian period

At the end of 1965, the *Queen Elizabeth* had an extensive refit in hopes of attracting more cruise passengers. As a result, the ship's career was extended by several years, and like the *Queen Mary,* her success was due as much to the public favor as it was to her profitability to Cunard.

But these two sea monsters were inevitably sentenced to death by the rise aviation and the preparation of the *Queen Elizabeth II.* The two ships passed each other for the last time in the mid-Atlantic on the night of September 25, 1967. The *Queen Mary* was making her final transatlantic crossing to Southampton before making for the quay at Long Island. The *Queen Elizabeth* was not taken out of service by Cunard until 1968. From here on, she would lead a more sedentary career. She set out on her final crossing under the British flag in October, 1968. Her new owner, a Florida based company, renamed her *Elizabeth* and planned to convert her into a floating hotel and visitors' attraction at Port Everglades. But the project never got off the ground following the failure of the company. The ship was bought in an auction by a Hong Kong Chinese, who

hoped to convert her into a floating university. The ship ended her life as the *Seawise University.* On January 9, 1972, she was destroyed by fire and went down before the refit was complete. The *Queen Elizabeth* was decidedly British all the way.

Length: 314 meters
(1029 feet)
Width: 36 meters
(118 feet)
Tonnage: 83,673 tons
Speed: 29 knots
Passengers: 2,273
Crew: 1,296 men

FOOLING THE ENEMY

The *Queen Elizabeth* had not been completed when war was declared in September 1939, and her dry dock had to be vacated to make way for military vessels. If not the longest, this ship was at least the heaviest ever built. In view of the conflict and to ensure the optimum conditions for her launch, it was vital to take advantage of high tides that only occurred twice a year. It was therefore essential to keep to the date of February 26, even if the ship was not completely finished. Her maiden voyage was made with all lights switched off, after the liner had been equipped with demagnetizing devices to deflect mines. In the morning of March 2, 1940, the *Queen Elizabeth* set off from the mouth of the Clyde for New York.

How did she escape the German submarines and aircraft? By making them think that the new liner would depart from Southampton. Intense activity was deployed on this part of the south coast, whose quays were filled with crates supposedly for loading on to the new giant of the seas. To prevent her departure, the German Air Force sent bombers over with typical German precision. At that very moment, the *Queen Elizabeth* was on her way to the United States, having already completed the most dangerous part of her crossing close to the British coast, which was under close surveillance by the enemy.

The Queen Elizabeth prepares to dock. The anchor is out and the red and white flag on the port side indicates the presence of a pilot on board.

101

FROM ONE PRESIDENT TO ANOTHER

This ship with such a stormy destiny is noteworthy for bearing the names of two shipping company presidents. She was first named the *Willem Ruys,* in honor of a descendant of the founder of Rotterdamsche Lloyd, who managed the company until he was shot by the Germans and whose surname was the same the firm's founder. The *Achille Lauro* was named after the serving president of the Lauro Line, when he was mayor of Naples.

Left: The Achille Lauro flying the white star on a light grey background of the Lauro Line. The ultramarine of her hull sether apart from other liners of the time, whose hulls were usually white.

THE HIJACKING OF THE *ACHILLE LAURO*

In October, 1985, the liner was engaged on a ten day cruise. A landing in Alexandria was scheduled in order to allow passengers to visit Cairo before rejoining the ship at Port Said. More than half the passengers took advantage of this, but some preferred to stay on board to relax and enjoy her amenities. During this trip, the vessel was taken hostage by five Palestinian terrorist commandoes. It was the first time in shipping history that such a hijack had taken place. It cost the life of an American Jewish tourist, Leon Klinghoffer, who did not take the terrorists' threats seriously enough. The group ordered a member of the crew to throw the corpse overboard, together with the handicapped victim's wheel chair. The terrorists obtained permission from the Egyptian authorities to leave the territory without harassment. When the liner arrived in Port Said, the terrorists got into a tugboat and treated themselves to a victory-lap around the harbor to the applause of the dockworkers. But the Americans were not disposed to abandon the game. They forced the airplane transporting the terrorists down over Sicily. In retaliation the Egyptian government detained the liner. The *Achille Lauro* had to suffer once more the repercussions of a crisis which had a profound effect on American-Egyptian relations.

Humiliation on Sea

Length: 192,4 meters (631 feet)
Width: 25.1 meters (82 feet)
Tonnage: 21,119 tons
Speed : 24.6 knots
Passengers: 900
Crew: 400 men

At the end of the thirties, the Netherlands had only one superliner, the *Nieuw Amsterdam*. A start was made on a new ship in January, 1939, which would enable Rotterdamsche Lloyd to compete with the British and German ships, and in particular the *Oranje*, a 20,000 ton liner launched four months earlier by Nederladsche SB Mij, a Dutch rival on the East Indies route. Rotterdamsche Lloyd, founded in 1839, was breaking new ground by ordering a ship whose lifeboats were not located on the upper deck but on a level with the hull.

The outbreak of war set back the launch of the ship, which had become the target of reprisals. While still in dock, she was bombed by the Germans, who decided to continue building her for their own use. During the Second World War, she was sabotaged by the Dutch resistance, bombed by the Royal Air Force, then evacuated and scuppered by the Germans. When peace returned, it was decided to put her into service despite the damage she had suffered. Her completion was considered a national priority.

Red, white and blue

On December 2, 1947, she set out on her maiden voyage to Batavia. All too soon, though, changes in the political climate dimmed the hopes placed in her by the company. Indonesia became independent in 1949, which led to a fall in passenger traffic on the route. In 1953, she collided with her rival, the *Oranje*.

The liner was then put on the New York route, and later the Canada route, before serving New Zealand via the Suez Canal. Eventually, she was incorporated into the same conglomerate as her competitor. But because of the drop in passenger traffic, both vessels were sold to the same Italian owner in 1964.

Green, white and red

Because payment was delayed, her new owner did not take possession of the ship until December, 1964. The Lauro Line undertook the reconfiguration of the liner, now called the *Achille Lauro*, in the shipyards of Palermo. But in August, 1965, just before delivery, a fire caused by an explosion delayed her entry into service until the spring of

1966. She once again served the Australian route until a new fire broke out in May of 1972, in the port of Genoa, where she was laid up again for five months.

On April 28, 1975, she sank a Lebanese ship, the *Youssef,* in the Dardanelles Straits, which cost several lives. The same year, the theft of a whole cargo by one-armed bandits destined for South Africa brought discredit on the company's directors.

In December, 1981, she was victim of a fire once again. In 1982, she was seized by the authorities as her owners had not paid their port duties. Returning from a cruise, she was stopped for several months in Tenerife before she could return to Genoa, where she was laid up because of company debts.

In 1985, the Lauro Line amalgamated with the Chandris Line. On October 7, in a terrorist hijack, the liner sadly entered the history books. She returned eight days later to her home port.

She took the Swiss flag in 1987, becoming the property of the Star Lauro Company. Her cruising career came to an end in the seas off Somalia, on December 2, 1994, with a fire that burned for three days. 1,087 survivors were picked up and three people died.

THE FRENCH ORIENTAL ROUTES

Operated by Messageries Maritimes, the routes to the Far East and the Levant were served by medium-sized, luxuriously decorated liners. History especially recalls the magnificence of the *Champollion* and the *Mariette Pacha* in Egyptian style, or the *Athos,* whose dining room was adorned with a painting by the famous marine artist, Sandy Hook. There was also the *Andre Lebon,* which in 1923 picked up survivors of the Tokyo earthquake, including the French ambassador, Paul Claudel. Messageries Maritimes carried on until the closure of the South American route, which it had operated for a decade, and the Oriental routes. In 1974, it merged with Transat. Renamed the Compagnie General Maritime, they decided to concentrate on freight operations.

This company card is modeled after a painting by the marine artist, Albert Brenet.

"LA MARSEILLAISE" EN RIVIÈRE DE SA

L'INDOCHINE ET L'EXTRÊME-ORIENT PAR LES MES

Length: 180.8 meters
(593 feet)
Width: 23 meters (75 feet)
Tonnage: 17,408 tons
Speed: 20.5 knots
Passengers: 673
Crew: 100 men

GERIES MARITIMES

The Glorious Days of Empire

It all began in completely surrealist circumstances with the launch on June 8, 1944, two days after the Allied landings in Normandy, of a liner ordered in 1939 and named the *Maréchal Pétain*. In the annals of merchant shipping, no naming could have been more inopportune. The first stage of her evolution was to give her a more acceptable name. *La Marseillaise* seemed appropriate in the euphoria of the Liberation, and considering Marseilles would be the home port of the ship sailing the Far East route. Between the liner's launch and her delivery there was a five-year delay. The finishing work on the ship, started in 1947, was spread out over two years at the La Ciotat Shipyards.

With this liner, which began service on June 30, 1949, Messageries Maritimes took delivery of their first new vessel since the Second World War. It was of an extremely elegant design and distinguished by a double pair of anchors. This medium-sized ship, with decorations worthy of her illustrious predecessors, had room for 673 passengers—half of them in steerage, including soldiers on leave and minor civil servants serving in Indo-China.

The independence of France's possessions in South East Asia had serious consequences for Messageries Maritimes. It meant the depletion of a large portion of her clientele on a route which now terminated at Yokohama, in a Japan which had few relations with Europe. In 1956, the liner was put on the Marseilles-Beirut route via Pireus and Alexandria. The Suez expedition at the end of that year precipitated her destiny under the French flag. She served as a hospital ship, but once the crisis was over, she was affected by Nasser's closure of the Suez Canal.

Her occasional troop transports to Algeria, where the struggle for independence was mounting, no longer justified her place in the Messageries Maritimes' fleet. So in February, 1957, after less than eight years of civilian service, she was handed over to Arosa Lines, which put her on the Bremerhaven-New York route and on cruises under the name *Arosa-Sky*. But at the end of 1958, she was resold to Italian owners, Costa Armatori.

Everything pointed to the *Bianca C*, as she was now known, becoming the jewel in a fleet of cruise liners: elegant lines, luxurious fittings, a yacht-like shape underlined by her white hull, a moderate speed and a capacity raised to more than 1,000 passengers. All this promised a long and successful career, but for a fire which sank her in October, 1961, after an explosion in the engine rooms.

During her 12 years in service, this ship had had three owners, four names, sailed on three routes (in addition to servicing cruises from New York) and experienced armed conflicts and their repercussions. Designed before the Second World War and the victim of the unstable post-war international relations, she became in some respects the unfortunate torch of a declining world order.

The Little Model Sisters

The liners *Flandre* and *Antilles* were representatives of the new economic situation that surfaced at the end of hostilities.

After the Second World War, Transat ordered two medium-sized liners from different shipyards. The company's aim was to make good the shortage of liners on the Central America route as a result of war losses. But the specifications also made provision for using the liners either for cruises or on the North Atlantic route, whose fleet had also been badly affected by the conflict. These sister ships were delivered in 1952 and 1953, respectively. The first, the *Flandre,* was launched at Dunkerque on October 31, 1951, and enjoyed a career twice as long as her sister ship.

Perfect stability

Originally, she was intended for the West Indies and Central America route, but during her construction, Transat's directors decided to put her on the North Atlantic route, an outcome they had envisaged. After modification, the *Flandre* would show how perfectly adaptable she was to different types of operations. Configured to transport 727 passengers with a crew of 405, the *Flandre* set off on her maiden voyage on July 23, 1952, after trials which proved her perfect stability, due to the special design of her propellers. However, her career started badly, as she had boiler and electrical problems and had to finish the crossing with the assistance of tugs. She was laid up for nine months while her teething problems were rectified. Afterwards, she fulfilled all the hopes her owners had placed in her, all the more so since they had made provision for some of the first-class and tourist cabins—accommodating up to 100 passengers—to become interchangeable. The *France's* entry into service, however, led to a change of use. The *Flandre* joined her sister ship on the West Indies route after her hull was repainted white. In 1968, Transat sold her to Italian owners, Costa Armatori, who undertook a complete overhaul, raising her funnel and making her a single-class ship. She served under the Italian flag for nearly 20 years as the *Carla C,* and later, six months before being sold, the *Carla Costa*.

A fine reputation

During the course of her French and Italian careers, this liner earned her place in the history of merchant shipping, due to her reputation for high standards which she maintained among a varied clientele, and the satisfaction she offered them.

In 1992, she was sold to a Greek owner who operated her under the name *Pallas Athena,* whose home port was Piraeus. There she caught fire at the start of the tourist season, sinking in shallow water after being towed out of port. The fire, combined with her stay underwater, caused too much damage for repairs to be considered.

FLANDRE
Length: 182.8 meters (600 feet)
Width: 24.4 meters (80 feet)
Tonnage: 20,469 tons
Speed: 23.8 knots
Passengers: 727
Crew: 405 men

ANTILLES
Length: 182.8 meters (600 feet)
Width: 24.4 meters (80 feet)
Tonnage: 19,828 tons
Speed: 23.8 tons
Passengers: 727
Crew: 405 men

THE FLANDRE

The *Flandre*, which entered service in 1952, was not the first liner to bear this name. In 1914, Transat launched a 146 meter (48 foot) long, 9,159 ton liner of the same name. Her career on the South American route, and later in West Indies, was interrupted by a service record in two world wars. She was decorated with the Military Cross before being sunk by a mine in September, 1940.

THE CRUISE SHIP ENJOYS HERSELF

This liner left a very good reputation behind over the course of 24 years under the French and Italian flags. Indeed, a trip on the *Carla C* inspired an American passenger to write a pleasant and humorous novel entitled *The Cruise Ship Enjoys Herself*, which recreated the atmosphere and the little events she observed during her stay.

THE ANTILLES
1953 - 1971

Built at Brest, *Antilles* benefited from the same basic design as her sister ship, the *Flandre*. She was distinguished by a white hull (the *Flandre's* hull was black when she sailed the North Atlantic route), a funnel three meters (10 feet) taller (from 1956 onwards) and by boilers which, despite their greater fragility, did not cause any of the problems the *Flandre* encountered at the start of her career. Transferred to the West Indies, she left Le Havre for the last time on November 25, 1970. She should have arrived at Pointe à Pitre the following January, but she ran aground on January 8, 1971, near the island of Moustique in the Grenadines. As a result of the damage, the fuel oil saturated the wooden floor of the boiler room, causing a fire which could not be put out. The crew managed to evacuate the 150 passengers, who were picked up by the *Queen Elizabeth II*, then on a cruise. The hull broke up a month an a half later and remained in the shallow waters for several years before being sold.

VIEW OF THE INTERIOR

The *United States* was a liner whose design had been dictated by the imperatives of fire prevention. The captain liked to persuade people that no part of it was likely to catch fire. He even placed a lighted cigarette on a blanket to desmonstrate that the fire risks were nil. Despite the almost exclusive use of non-flammable materials, the decor of the ship was not at all dreary. Decoration was sparse and very American in taste, and in a style so typical to the fifties. Indeed, the *United States* was a very comfortable and luxurious liner. Her areas were less imposing than those on the liners of the interwar years, but this option was better suited to the needs of a liner comprising three classes, and to the economic situation that had been created by the end of the Second World War.

END OF A JOURNEY

The *United States* made her last crossing in November, 1969, having transported not a single soldier, and stayed at anchor on the quay of oblivion until 1992. In that year, she was bought by a Turkish owner who planned to organize cruises in the Caribbean. The first shipyard dealt with cleaning out the ship, which at the time was lined entirely with asbestos. The work was completed in the Crimea, but alarmed at the huge expense of the conversion, the owner resold the liner to the Marmara Marine Company. On January 27, 1997, she was seized by the American authorities for nonpayment of debt. Since then, she has been waiting at a quay in Philadelphia for a reconfiguration which would enable her to start out on a new career. Will this happen one day soon?

The Idle Meteor

Length: 301.8 meters
(990 foot)
Width: 31 meters
(102 feet)
Tonnage: 53,329 tons
Speed: 38.3 knots
Passengers: 1,928
Crew: 1,093 men

The *United States* is the liner which best symbolizes the turning point that the fifties represented in passenger transport.

This ship would never have seen the light of day if the world had not been divided by the Cold War.

She was, above all, the result of a political decision by the United States Federal Government. It may seem surprising that the U. S., which occupied a secondary position in passenger shipping for a century, should decide to subsidise such a ship.

It was the exemplary service of the two Queens during the Second World War that led the Amercian Admiralty to seek a way of transporting the maximum number of soldiers in the minimum amount of time. The military establishment persuaded the government to order an immense liner which could be converted into an ultrarapid troop transport in record time, and which in peacetime would be the most luxurious amd comfortable liner in the world.

In 1946, the Government placed an order for this monster with William Francis Gibbs, a very celebrated naval architect. After the end of the Second World War, he had been responsible for the reconversion of the *Leviathan* (formerly the *Vaterland*) as a liner, the U. S. having used her as a troop transport after her seizure in April, 1917. At the age of 60, he regarded this commission as the crowning point of his career. But at the same time, it was a new experience for him, since by reason of the ship's dual purpose, he had to work closely with the American navy, maintaining secrecy regarding the construction of the hull and the characteristics of the propellers.

Gibbs counted on gaining speed by lightening the vessel's structure and lining it with aluminium. This material enabled him to assuage the near-obsessional fear he had of fire. The man was legendary for eliminating the slightest piece of furniture or equipment made of wood. He readily accepted the kitchen's butcher's block, but it was only after se-veral heated discussions that he gave up his plan for an aluminium piano and agreed to tolerate the more traditional instrument.

Although he managed to lighten the ship and give her better stability, Gibbs' use of aluminium caused the building costs to rocket when compared with more typical solutions. As a result, the *United States* was the most expensive ship ever built. Her construction cost $80 million, with a Government contribution of $45 million.

The most expensive liner, but also the fastest, she is said to have attained 40 knots during her trials. This was confirmed by her performance on her inaugural crossing, beginning on July 3, 1952, which she completed 10 hours faster than the *Queen Mary*, which had held the Blue Riband since 1938.

It is on the strength of this achievement, in which the Americans had not participated for 100 years, that the *United States* began a transatlantic career, during which she had the honor, with the *France,* of carrying the *Mona Lisa.* However, her last years of service were full of warning signs against the inadequacy of the economic environment. The liner suffered from very high labor costs, and especially from the competition of airlines, which in 1967 took 92% of the passenger traffic between Europe and the United States.

109

UNITED STATES

The Sinking of the Admiral

After little more than three years of service, the *Andrea Doria,* like the *Titanic,* entered legend with a spectacular sinking. Yet this liner had certain trump cards which would have ensured her a long life, had not fate decided otherwise.

After the disaster of the Second World War, Italy was without her finest ships, the *Roma, Augustus, Rex* and *Conte di Savoia,* which had all been retired to the bottom of the sea. She resumed passenger services with smaller boats to maintain a presence on the Atlantic. In 1949, boosted by the development of tourism, the Compagnie Nationale Italia obtained subsidies from the government, enabling them to order a luxury liner from the Ansaldo shipyards the same year.

The ship that set out on her maiden voyage on January 14, 1953, revived the great tradition of elegance on Italian vessels. She aroused a strong sense of patriotism and immediately gained favour with her new clientele. Following a more southerly route to reach the United States, she was the first to have three open air swimming pools, one for each class of passengers. The first-class saloon was adorned with a full-scale statue of Andrea Doria, the 16th-century Genoan admiral who passed from Francis I's service to that of Charles V, and to whom the victory against the Turks in 1519 was credited. The ship was placed under the command of Piero Calamai, the best captain in the Italian fleet who had been sailing since the age of 19.

It was on the evening of July 25, 1956, that the ship's destiny took a sudden turn. In the approach to the American coast, which would end the nine day crossing, there appeared a thick fog. The *Stockholm,* a small Swedish liner, was approaching in the opposite direction after setting out in clear weather. The collision that followed was characterized by the fact that it happened with the full knowledge of both crews, since both vessels were equipped with radar.

On board the *Andrea Doria,* Captain Calamai took the decision to pass the *Stockholm* on the starboard side, contrary to the rules of navigation on the high seas. But he had thought that the other ship was on that side of him. When the two ships came in sight of each other, it was too late to avoid a collision. The side of the Andrea Doria was rammed at 23.10 hours and the ship immediately started to list.

The collision took the lives of five people on the *Stockholm* and 47 on the *Andrea Doria.* Despite serious damage to her fiber glass stem, the Swedish liner stayed afloat and returned to port under her own steam. She even took part in the rescue, launching her lifeboats onto the sea. Thanks to a radio link, news was rapidly picked up by the *Ile de France,* commanded by Raoul de Beaudean, who came to rescue the majority of the survivors.

Length: 213.4 meters (44 feet)
Width: 27.5 meters (90 feet)
Tonnage: 29,083 tons
Speed: 23 knots
Passengers; 1,241
Crew: 563 men

THE RESPONSIBILITY

How could such a collision take place? The fog which enveloped the *Andrea Doria* does not explain everything, since the ship had enough equipment on board to effect a manoeuvre when visibility was lacking. In the end, it was put down to the lack of experience of a 26 year-old officer, who was the only person on watch on the *Stockholm* at the time of the collision, and to Captain Calamai's error in wanting to pass on the starboard side. One other factor could also explain the disaster. The *Andrea Doria*, which was then about 100 miles from New York, had used up almost all of her fuel oil reserve. To add weight and keep her balance, the crew should have filled her tanks with sea water. However, knowing that he had to undertake a return voyage that would give him only a short turnaround time in port, the captain had neglected to fill the tanks which would have needed to be emptied again, thus adding to the delay.

ITALY WITHOUT THE ANDREA DORIA

With the sinking of the *Andrea Doria* a nation's dream had faded. Her sister ship, the *Cristoforo Colombo*, which entered service in 1954, never aroused the same patriotic feeling. The Compagnie Italia's other two luxury ships, the *Michelangelo* and the *Raffaello*, took to the seas in 1965 for short careers under the Italian flag—10 years—because of fall in passenger traffic. These two longer vessels (276 meters, 905 feet) were operating in an economic climate increasingly dominated by air traffic, and they were too large to be put to alternative use on cruises. The *Stockholm*, which entered service in 1948, would later take the name *Italia Prima*, and would sail in turn under the East German and Norwegian flags.

UNDER THE SIGN OF THE ZODIAC

LItaly's best artists and designers worked on the *Andrea Doria* to make her the most worthy successor to the *Rex*. A deluxe suite on her was regarded as a model of elegance and good taste. She featured the twelve signs of the zodiac, and there was also a religious motif—a regular practice on Italian liners—in the form of a portrait of the Madonna. However, in deference to the occupants' faith, or lack there of, it could easily be concealed behind two sliding panels.

The double agent

Launched in 1958, in the presence of Queen Juliana, the *Rotterdam* was the last superliner to be built in the nation's shipyards for the Holland america Line, which was later taken over by foreign companies.

The *Rotterdam* was one of the most luxurious and comfortable ships of her generation. Her clientele liked her a great deal, in particular for the abundant use of precious woods, her twelve passenger decks, her two dining rooms joined by a wide vestibule designed for 900 diners, the grill room adjacent to each of them and, above all, the Ritz Carlton Room—a dance bar two decks high that could accommodate 250 people. The private areas gained similar favor with the public, which was not surprising since, for the first time, the owners had made early mockups of the cabins to test the reactions of their potential clientele.

This liner, which entered service in 1959, exuded an intimate, club-like atmosphere, to such an extent that clients would return year after year. Such customer loyalty, as well as her reputation for excellence, explains the commercial success that the *Rotterdam* enjoyed throughout her long career. To further facilitate her access, a special pier was built for her in the port of New York.

Cruises

Public approbation alone did not explain the liner's exceptional profitability for her owners. Her success was also due to the fact that she had been designed for dual uses. She could accommodate 1,456 passengers in two classes on her transatlantic crossings, or just 730 vacationers in first-class cruises. It was for this latter purpose that the *Rotterdam* was most used, holding the record for the largest number of round-the-world cruises.

In 1973, the Holland America Lijn was renamed Holland America Cruise and her head office was transferred to the United States. Since then she has merged with Carnival Cruise Lines, Inc. The *Rotterdam* continued her career on circular routes suited to the seasons: Alaska and Canada in summer, the Gulf of Mexico, the Caribbean and California in winter. The city of Rotterdam had planned to repatriate the ship and turn her into a museum and congress center, but they soon abandoned the idea. The liner was finally passed on to Premier Cruise Lines, and she continues to provide cruises under the name *Rembrandt*.

Length: 227,90 m
Width: 28,70 m
Tonnage : 38 645 tons
Cruising speed: 20,5 knots
Passagers: 1 456
Crew: 776 men

A PRONOUNCED SHAPE

The most striking aspect of the *Rotterdam* was the absence of funnels, which had been replaced by two exhaust shafts located at the same level at the back of the boat and joined horizontally by a pipe. One consequence of this was that the Holand America Lijn could never paint her colors—two green stripes with a yellow one in between—on a funnel in the traditional manner, so it was put on the superstructure of the deck. This innovation—more for aesthetic than technical reasons—caused great excitement among liner enthusiasts. As well, the idea of the two twin exhaust devices would be taken up by other companies, most notably on the *Eugenio C.*

I Don't Love You Either

This was a curious fate for a liner around which the expectations of a nation seemed to crystallize, as well as its contradictions. The ship, that was launched by General and Madame de Gaulle on May 11, 1960, would be the last great French passenger liner. It was also the longest to date.

"She has married the sea. Vive la France!" the President cried. The engagement had lasted a long time, but the marriage itself was quite short.

It was on July 25, 1956, the day the *Andrea Doria* was rammed, that the order to build her was signed after three years of discussion. The accession to the presidency of a man from Le Havre, René Coty, in early 1954, had not accelerated the decision-making. However, Transat needed to think of a replacement for the valiant *Ile de France,* whose running costs were becoming exorbitant. Their plan received financial support from the state, which eventually offered a subsidy of 76.6 million francs to compensate for the extra cost of having her built at the Penhoët Shipyards, rather than by rival companies.

Characterized by two funnels that were equipped with fins to prevent smoke from falling onto the deck, the *France* was inaugurated officially on January 11, 1962. Two days la-

ter, she left for her maiden cruise to the Canaries, passing in the Gulf of Gascony the *Liberté,* which was en route for the demolition yards of La Spezia.

France and after

On February 3, she was put on the North Atlantic route for the first time with 2,000 passengers on board, making a triumphant arrival in New York on February 8. She enjoyed an excellent reputation among her clientele, particularly for the excellence of her French cuisine. She continued her service on the North Atlantic route until 1972.

The *France's* career came to a halt in 1974, after transporting more than 700,000 passengers on regular service and on cruises. The commercial success of the liner was not replicated in terms of profitability, and the French Government was no longer prepared to offer an annual subsidy to offset the running costs. Faced with the pre-eminence of air transport and the consquences of the 1973 oil crisis, Transat announced that the ship would be laid up.

Thus began a litany of disasters. After being laid up at the end of the year, the *France* stayed in dock—a cumbersome symbol of national

pride that was unwilling to finance its ambitions. A Saudi Arabian, Akram Odjeh, bought her in 1977, keen to make her into a floating museum to house a part of his collection. This project did not materialize, most notably because the owner could not find a home port for the ship. She remained inactive for five years until she was resold in 1979 to the Norwegian owner Kloster. After converting her engines to reduce running costs, she now undertakes cruises bearing the name *Norway.*

When she returns to French terirtorial waters, however, she assumes her original name. Her presence always arouses great interest with the general public, which quickly evaporates when the ship takes to the sea again for foreign shores. The *Norway,* has definitely become naturalized.

THE *FRANCE* SEEN FROM INSIDE

The decoration of the *France* relied extensively on Formica, aluminium and composite materials. But the greatest novelty lay in the level of her fittings. The liner could accommodate around 2,000 passengers, three quarters of whom were tourist class. The organization of public spaces was now done longitudinally and no longer according to level, which gave everyone the impression of having the whole of a deck at his disposal. The decoration relied on the artists of the time, with works by Gromaire, Carzou, Picasso, Dufy and Dunoyer de Segonzac, for instance. The first class smoking room was adorned with a 17 meter tapestry by Picart Le Doux. The restaurants remained separate. The tourist class facility offered two sittings, while there was only one in the Chambord Room, which was reserved for first class clients.

THE *FRANCE* AS A CRUISE SHIP

The *France* undertook a number of cruises that stand out in the history of shipping. The Imperial Cruise in April of 1969 took *Napoleon I* as its theme. Her ports of call were the islands which marked the various stages in his career. The two round-the-world cruises, which took place from January to April, were a challenge for Transat, which was expected to provide the same quality of service at any point on the globe. Though the 1972 cruise was undeniably a success, the 1974 one that was undertaken after the oil crisis was less successful commercially, and operated at a loss.

A HEART STORY

Like the *Ile de France,* the *France* saved the lives of passengers on liners passing in her vicinity, particularly due to the operating theatre with which she was equipped. The ship made history in being the first to transmit by satellite the results of a passenger's electrocardiogram to French and American teams simultaneously, thus facilitating international collaboration for a patient who was being treated at sea.

THE *FRANCE*: A SCENE OF POLITICAL CONFLICT

From her conception, the *France* was the focus of bitter struggles between trade unions and the employers and government. On September 11, 1974, the *France* was immobilized by a section of the crew. The liner's fate aroused national interest, every side wanting to maintain operations without financing the deficit. While in nearly every British household there was a photo of the *Queen Mary*, the French had a less developed patriotic fiber. The government refused to give in, and the strike finished on October 10. The trade unions showed their strength for the last time when the ship was handed over the Norwegian Caribbean Lines. They demanded that the liner's conversion be undertaken in France, not Germany. Police intervention was necessary to enable to ship to leave Le Havre in August, 1979.

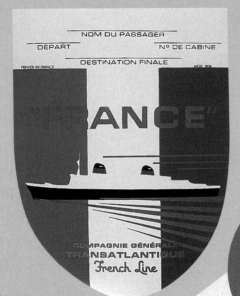

Menus.

Baggage tickets.

PAQUEBOT
"FRANCE"
PREMIÈRE CLASSE

Le Pamplemousse Surprise Rafraîchi

Le Caviar Givré de la Caspienne

La Crème Champenoise à la

Le Homard des Cor

DE GRASSE

Chef des Cuisines :

SAMEDI 15 JUILLET 1972

DU

Noisette d'Agneau des Causses Fleuriste

Salade Allan

Dîner

Olives Vertes - Olives Noires - Céleri en Branche
Beurre de Bernay d'Orange
Jus de Tomate d'Amour, d'Orange
Caviar de Russie Givré - Canapés City
Salade Frasgra. Coupe de Crevettes Cocktail
Pâté de Veau et Jambon en Croûte
Melon Cranshaw Rafraîchi au Citron

Velouté de Légumes Rivernais
Consommé Double Ox-Tail
Soupe à l'Oignon Gratinée au Gruyère

Œufs Pochés Bénédict - Œufs au Plat Chasse
Médaillon de Saumon Rose
Saint-Pierre Froid Sauce

Mercredi 13 Juin 1951

Menu

LUNCH
Hors-d'Œuvre à la Française
Potage Saint-Germain
Saint-Germain Soup
Fine Green Peas à la Française
Coquilled Peas à l'Anglaise
Coquille Soul Mornai au Feu de Bois
Broiled Potato Neuf Potatoes au Feu de Bois
Mashed Potatoes Cheese Potatoes
Baba au Rhum - Marmelute Potatoes
Vanilla Ice Cream
Assorted Fruits
Orange Juice - Milk

DINNER
Iced Grapefruit
Savoy Cocktail
Soup
Chicken à la VIrmonnaise
Eggs Frid à l'Anglaise
Mashed potate à l'Anglaise
Carret Vichy
Roast Spring Lamb à la Broche
Mashed Potatoes au Gratin
Baked Potatoes
Gruyay Cheese

Chicorée Fraîche Braisée à Fu
Haricots Verts Sauté aux Fin
Beignets de Maïs Fraîs Sauce
Riz Pilaw
Pommes Idaho au Four - Pomme
Pommes Paille - Pommes Da

Foie de Veau Laitier Grillé au B

Dindonneau du Vermont Rôti aux Alt
Jambon de Paris - Jambon de Westph
Jambon de Parme - Jambon de Virginie Clouté
Poulet de Grain à la Gelée - Quartier d'Agneau
Longe de Veau Mayonnaise - Pied d'Aloyau au
Terrine de Foie Gras Jandaise
Langue Sal

DÉJEUNER
Hors-d'Œuvre à la Française
Potage Saint-Germain
Œuf au Plat à l'Anglaise
Pois Poêlé à la Française
Pois Verts et au Beurre
Pommes au Feu de Bois

THE CORNISH FISHING TOWN OF LOOE, FROM THE SEA

PÂTES
GRILLADE
(10 minutes)
RÔTI
BUFFET FROID

Salade de Scarole aux Bette
Camembert - Brie
Bourslaze
Mimolette - Tête-de-

SALADES
FROMAGES

Crème Mentonn
Coquille Sain
Assiette

ENTREMETS

Café Franca
Café Sanka

L'ARCHE

L. EN MER

L'ARCHE DE NOÉ

Menu

Stirring ustensils
and coasters.

CUNARD
Queen Elizabeth 2

MS Europa

A scarf provided to
emigrants by HAPAG at the
beginning of the century.

Hamburg-Amerika Linie

Przeprawa pasażerów okrętami pospie...skich

prawie do WSZ...

117

...oło

DEUTSCHLAND

Hamburgu, Bahnho...

"FRANCE"

An ashtray from the France.

THE SWEDISH TRADITION

The Swedish merchant navy was noted particularly for its loyalty to a limited number of names: the *Kungsholm, Stockholm, Gripsholm,* etc. The *Kungsholm,* which entered service in 1966, of course conforms to this tradition. Although the Svenska Amerika Linjen was founded in 1915, it did not prosper until after the First War. In 1922, the company bought the *Noordam* from the Holland America Lijn and renamed her the *Kungsholm.* In 1928, and then in 1953, it took possession of two new liners bearing the same name. The second of these, which was sold to NDL, became the *Europa,* also a traditional name in that owner's fleet.

The beauty of the devil

Length: 201.2 meters (660 feet)
Width: 26.5 meters (87 feet)
Tonnage: 26,678 tons
Speed: 21 knots
Passengers: 713
Crew: 438 men

The *Kungsholm,* was the fourth ship to bear this name.

Her construction symbolized the end of an era. She was one of the last ships, along with the *Queen Elizabeth II,* to leave the John Brown shipyard on the Clyde estuary near Glasgow. She was also the last superliner to be delivered to the Svenska America Linjen, which was very much at the forefront in regard to the modernity of its fleet, which ceased trading in 1975.

Miss Sweden

Given very elegant lines, the *Kungsholm IV* was distinguished by two majestic funnels with twin deflectors (nicknamed "firemen's hats"), the principle of which had been formulated before the Second World War by Francis Gibbs, the man responsible for the conversion of the *Leviathan,* as well as the design of the *America,* launched one day before Hitler's invasion of Poland, and of the *United States.*

The *Kungsholm* underwent her trials in November, 1965 before setting off on her maiden voyage from Göteborg in April, 1966. She served the New York route via Southampton until 1975, when she was sold to Flagship Cruises, which put her on cruises from the United States. This type of work suited the *Kungsholm* well, since her fittings were originally designed to satisfy both regular passengers and a vacationers on pleasure trips.

A facelift

In 1978, the ship changed hands. She was sold to P&O for the Princess Cruise Line. Her modernization was undertaken by the Vulkan Yards at Bremen, where she was reconfigured for exclusive use as a cruise ship. Unfortunately, her elegant shape was ruined in order to make more space on the upper deck. The ship lost one of her funnels and the remaining one acquired an ungraceful cone shape.

In this less attractive form, and renamed the *Sea Princess,* she took to the sea once more, first for cruises to the Pacific and Asia. Nowadays, departing from Southampton, she undertakes cruises on the Norwegian fjords, the Baltic Sea and the Mediterranean. The liner spirit has gone, but at least the ship continues her career—under the name *Victoria.*

119

The Queen Elizabeth II
before the 1986 overhaul.
The funnel is still white and
will then became red.

The last of the Queens

Length: 293.7 meters
(893 feet)
Width: 32 meters
(105 feet)
Tonnage: 65,863 tons
Speed: 28.5 knots
Passengers: 2,005
Crew: 906 men

Here is a liner caught between tradition and modernity, is the last of her line, and still sails the Atlantic between Europe and the United States from time to time. She is traditional because she was built at the John Brown shipyard in Glasgow, from where her glorious ancestors emerged, and also because she is invested with the title of the queen who named her at her launch on September 20, 1967. However, much had changed since the appearance of the other two Queens, and at by end of the sixties the idea "small is beautiful" became popular. Because of this, Cunard could now claim to have the fastest and largest liners.

With her 293.7 meters, (893 feet) she is 20 meters (70 feet) shorter than the *Queen Elizabeth,* and weighs 15,000 tons less than the *Queen Mary,* as well as being 4 knots slower. She is less powerful than the *France,* which used up to 160,000 horse power.

But she is modern because, while lowering their ambitions, the owners obtained the liner they wanted: a ship designed for cruises which could also undertake transatlantic crossings. She was small enough to pass through the Panama Canal: sufficiently steady, thanks to her anti-roll stabilizers, to ensure passenger comfort; sufficiently well-equipped and able to preoccupy the passengers (with Turkish baths, saunas, panoramic restaurants, a shopping mall, and four swimming pools); and sufficiently fast to attain 28.5 knots in service, with a top speed of 32 knots.

Externally, the *Queen Elizabeth II* is noteworthy for her single, narrow funnel in two parts; an exhaust conduit surrounded by two ventilators and a single hollow mast which serves to release the smoke from the kitchens.

Delivered in 1969, the *Queen Elizabeth II* began her commercial life on May 2, from Southampton bound for New York. Following the tradition of the Queens, she conveyed British troops during the Falkland War, which led to the fall of the Argentinian dictatorship and in which Prince Andrew, the Queen's son, participated.

At the end of 1986, she underwent a long overhaul at Bremerhaven. In addition to a refit, the system of propulsion was changed. The *QE2,* as she is familiarly known, became the largest ship ever to be propelled by diesel motors. The funnel was replaced by a larger one, albeit lower and lighter, causing fewer smoke discharges on the deck.

And today?

She is still sailing. In addition to cruises, she still makes regular transatlantic crossings from Southampton. In this sense, she is the last of the true liners, although the route is sometimes served by European ships in the process of repositioning, in order to sail with a passenger load to America where cruise travellers await them.

On the transatlantic route, it is England who has the last word. It is still possible, in this very British way, to reach New York in several days on a crossing which, now as before, remains timeless.

121

A poet and her sisters

Both in her design and her operational characteristics, the *Alexandr Pushkin* is a medium-sized liner, representing perfectly a superpower that wishes to appear aimiable and mighty in turn.

The construction of a series of liners of around 20,000 tons came underway at the Mathias Thessen shipyards in Wismar in the early sixties. These ships, each bearing the name of a poet or writer, were distinguished by a single funnel in the form of a truncated cone. They had good lines and a decent level of comfort, and were likely to attract a middle-class clientele for transatlantic crossings as well as cruise passengers.

Soviet on Sea

This series of liners had certain, typically Soviet, features. Immediately noticeable was the lifting gear on the deck, which was of considerable size and power when compared with those on other liners. This revealed the Kremlin's ulterior motive of haying the facility to transport armored vehicles.

Another notable feature was the large proportion of female staff. However, concern for equality between men and women does not appear to be the main reason. In reality, this mixing the sexes protected members of the crew from the desire to strike up a relationship with passengers of the opposite sex. Because of this, the crew would leave the ship together at the various ports of call, and not have to mingle with the passengers. Apart from this, the liners had features which had existed earlier on the liners of foreign companies, but had since been largely abandoned. For example, cabins for six people and three faucets in the bathroom shower for hot water, cold water and sea water were provided. The Soviet liners were the only ones to retain such an economical but outdated system.

The *Aleksandr Pushkin* operated on the transatlantic route between Leningrad (now St. Petersburg) and Montreal, with stops at Copenhagen and London until 1975. At this stage she was one of just three liners operating a North Atlantic service. Afterwards, with her hull repainted white, she was chartered for cruises by British, French and German tour companies specializing in the USSR. Throughout, the crew remained Soviet, but was supplemented by entertainers, hostesses and chefs from the countries which had chartered her.

In 1991, the *Aleksandr Pushkin* was sold to a Greek owner who converted her at shipyards in Piraeus. Renamed the *Marco Polo,* the ship was equipped with RADOM, her lifing gear was given a more civilian height, and her hull was repainted black. She continued to do cruise work under her new flag until 1998, when she was sold to the Norwegian Cruise Line for the same use.

Length: 176.3 meters (578 feet)
Width: 23.6 meters (77 feet)
Tonnage: 19,860 tons
Speed: 20.5 knots
Passengers: 750
Crew: 220 men

122

STALIN STARTS WITH SECOND HAND GOODS

The First World War and the 1917 Revolution suddenly brought to an end the great efforts (begun by Czar Nicholas II) to build a merchant navy and extend the rail network. Until 1940, the Soviet merchant navy was under represented with small ships built abroad. The end of the Second World War, however, gave Stalin an opportunity to build up a merchant fleet at minimal cost. He did this at the expense of a vanquished Germany (which provided 80% of his naval booty) and also called on sister nations (such as Poland and Romania), and even the partisans of countries not yet liberated. In this way, the Little Father managed to acquire ships from the Spanish Republicans in return for Soviet aid to the anti-Francoists during the Spanish Civil War.

... AND HIS SUCCESSORS PAY AGAIN

Between 1958 and 1964, the Soviets renewed their merchant fleet by taking delivery of the largest series of liners ever ordered. Requests for twenty two completely identical ships were placed with the Mathias Thesen shipyards in Wismar (formerly East Germany). The enforced collaboration with the older brother enabled the latter to provide at low cost a fleet of small (around 5,000 tons) yet very successful ships. It was during the time of Kruschev's successor, Brezhnev, that construction was carried out on the five liners, named after poets and writers, at the same East German shipyard. The USSR remembered the successful evacuation of East Prussia by German liners. The Soviet liners would serve to transport troops and technical advisers in different military interventions, most notably in African countries. There was never a clear distinction between civilian and military naval personnel. Some naval staff were rewarded for good conduct by finishing their lengthy military service on cruise ships.

THE OTHER SISTERS

The five sister ships were designed to operate either on the North Atlantic route or on cruises. The three home ports of the Soviet liners were Leningrad, Odessa and Sebastapol in Russia and the Ukraine. The Baltic Republics' ports could only take liners of small tonnage. The *Ivan Franko* and the *Aleksandr Pushkin* served first on the Canadian route, departing from Leningrad, before being used for cruises. The *Mikhail Lermontov*, which entered service in 1972, was also employed on cruises, except for one year in 1973 when she sailed the Leningrad-New York route. She was lost in 1986 in the seas off New Zealand after striking reefs. The *Shota Rustaveli* and the *Taras Shevchenko* were immediatedly deployed on cruises organized by foreign travel agencies. The break-up of the Soviet Union in 1991 led to a sharing out of the merchant fleet, most of which returned to the Russian Federation and the Ukraine.

TOMORROW

Gradually, the passenger liners still in service have been converted into cruise ships. Yet there is a notable exception, the *Queen Elizabeth II*, which was designed both for regular crossings and for pleasure cruises. She continues to make a few round trips each year between Southampton and New York, thus carrying on the liner tradition. It was in the sixties that ships designed expressly for cruises first appeared. This form of leisure activity is actually quite old, beginning at the end of the 19th century, following the example of P & O, when Albert Ballin secured a financial return for some HAPAG liners during the low season. But the development of international travel and the increase in living standards gave rise to a younger and more active clientele. In parallel with this, liners are becoming more and more like floating hotels. So what has changed? The loss of national pride, since the cruise liners for the most part fly the flags of countries which are not economic powerhouses, and the service is provided by a cosmopolitan staff. It can also be attributed to the complete separation of admiralties from shipping companies. However, there has been a return to some features which recall the great age of the liner, such as the black or dark blue hulls as in the days of coal, and also a fascination for funnels, which are no longer symbols of prestige, but a pole of attraction especially for panoramic bars, for which they are often the center.

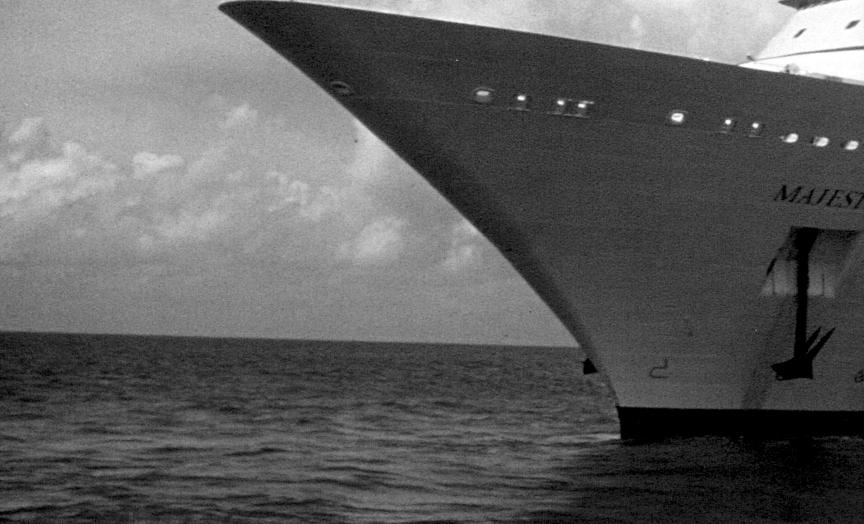

Above: *The* Wind Song *in French Polynesia.*

Above: *The* Wind Song *and the* Queen Elizabeth II.

126

Small is beautiful

ove: The Paul Gauguin and Below: a Club Med in Sydney.

In the market for water leisure, two opposing trends can been found; the first is for ships which are closer to yachts; the second is for designs of enormous proportions. In both cases, the customer requirements are more precisely targeted for today, where time is precious and the aim is not gain from it, but to spend it to the best effect on one's areas of interest.

Yacht liners

Some cruises are served by liners which can accommodate a moderate number of passengers—between 300 and 700. But in contrast with the great age of liners, there is a trend to build small units with luxurious and standardized private rooms of a single class. The quality of the fittings and superstructures enable discriminating cruise enthusiasts to experience the exclusive atmosphere of an elite club. Some examples of these yacht liners are Cunard's *Sea Goddess,* Seabourn Cruise's three *Seabourn Prides,* the Silver, *the Radisson,* and the recently launched *Paul Gauguin.*

Sail liners

Sail liners are one of the most radical innovations of the last fifteen years, and fulfill one of Jean Claude Potier's dreams. This Frenchman, a former officer on passenger and cruise liners, worked with Karl Andren (a Finnish director of Circle Line, a company that offers tours around Manhattan), in order to conduct a marketing-survey directed at promoting ocean travel. With the arrival of cruise ships, marketing has long established its influence on liner design. It was as a result of these studies that an order was placed for the Wind series with the Ateliers and Chantiers du Havre at Graville.

The three liners, the *Wind Star,* the *Wind Song* and the *Wind Spirit* entered service in 1986, 1987 and 1988, respectively. They are most notable for the fact they are run entirely by computer, including the six sails which have a total surface area of 2,000 square metres, and are equipped with an auxiliary motor. The ships are small, 134 meters (440 feet) long, with 74 cabins. The completely identical *Wind Star* and *Wind Song* can accommodate 148 passengers in double cabins and a crew of 82, including service personnel. The *Wind star,* with some triple cabins, is designed to take 159 passengers.

This new concept of a sail liner later inspired the contruction of *Club Med I* and *Club Med II,* which at 187 meters (61 feet) are designed for a larger number of passengers (440). The *Club Med I* was later taken over by Wind Star Sail Cruise. Since then, she has been renamed *Wind Surf* and her passenger capacity has been considerably reduced.

The Paul Gauguin

Delivered in 1997, the *Paul Gauguin* is one of the most recent yacht liners. Built in the Chantier de l'Atlantique, she is 156.5 meters (513 feet) in length, weighs 15,900 tons and has 160 cabins.

She offers a perfect illustration of the internationalization of the world of pleasure cruises that has been evolving for some time. Her owners are Services et Transports, directed by Jean-Marc Poylo (who was responsible for building the two *Club Med* ships in collaboration with the vacation specialist whose name they bear). The ship is operated by the Radisson Group and is marketed in France by the Compagnie Maritime des Croisières.

The New Quest for Size

The current trend in building giant liners is the continuation of a movement which started some years ago. The recent entry into service of the new *Vision* series demonstrates clearly the trend towards building these giant liners in a series.

Royal Caribbean enjoyed considerable success with her South Seas series, comprising the *Sovereign of the Seas, Monarch of the Seas* and *Majesty of the Seas.* This success prompted the company to place an order with the Chantiers de l'Atlantique at Saint Nazaire for yet another series: the *Legend of the Seas, Splendour of the Seas, Rhapsody of the Seas* and *Vision of the Seas,* delivered in 1995, 1996, 1997 and 1998, respectively. Although belonging to the same series, the ships are actually pairs of twins. The *Vision of the Seas,* delivered on April 16, 1998, weighs 76,000 tons and is 279 meters (915 feet) long. She is designed to transport 2,417 passengers and 780 crew, including service personnel. P & O's *Grand Princess,* put into service in May, 1998, harks back to the sea monsters of the Belle Epoque. Built in Italy for a sum of 2.7 billion francs, she is the largest liner of all in terms of tonnage (109,000 tons), but her length (289 meters, 948 feet) does not attain the record set by the *France.* Designed to take 2,600 passengers and a crew of 1,100, this floating city is completely focused on leisure. The promenade deck, whose area is utilized to capacity, has a minigolf course with nine holes, a tennis court and two swimming pools. At the rear, there is also a discotheque served by an escalator. The lower decks offer public areas that cater to American tastes with a casino, a night club and an amphitheatre.

Above: Cruise liners in Miami.
Below: A closer look at the decks of the Grand Princess.

Below: The dimensions of the wheelhouse are the same as those on a liner
Below: The Grand Princess, *pictured here in Monaco, has a very special shape that is far removed from the typical liner style.*

The ship is destined to compete with the *Carnival Destiny.* This flagship of Carnival Cruise Lines is slightly smaller—101,000 tons, 272 meters (892 feet) long—but can take a larger number of passengers (3,360). She is most notable for having a swimming pool equipped with a waterslide—an unusual feature on a liner.

The Disney Cruise Corporation, an extension of the Disney leisure concept, placed an order in Italy for four ships, two of which are still under construction. The *Disney Magic,* which entered service in 1998, and the *Disney wonder* are twins of 85,000 tons each and over 280 metres (918 feet) in length. They have classic lines with navy blue hulls and two funnels. For the moment, the cruises are operated out of Florida. Despite the omnipresence of Walt Disney characters in the decoration and the activities offered to the 2,400 passengers, there has been a return to the Art Deco-style in the hall, which contrasts sharply to the atria of purely American inspiration which are found on most of the recent liners.

Mention must be made of the most luxurious liner ever conceived. This 85,000 ton ship, called the *World Residency,* is exceptional in that it is the first to be sold under a co-ownership scheme. The order was placed for her in Germany on April 30, 1998, for $545 million, and she is scheduled to enter service in April of 2001. The vessel will comprise 40 small residences of less than 100 square meters (1076 square feet) and 246 apartments of different areas, the largest being 387 square meters (4190 square feet) in extent. One can imagine the

130

Above: The Sun Princess *arriving at Fort Lauderdale, Florida. The tug accompanying her gives an idea of her size.*
Below: The Star Princess, *which has entered the P & O fleet as the* Arcadia.
Right: The swimming pool on the Grand-Princess.

benefits for passengers who can afford a second home for anywhere of between $600,000 and $800,000.
The Royal Caribbean Cruise Line is going ahead with her Eagle Project of three identical ships, the first of which entered service in 1999. These are real monsters, weighing 142,000 tons, a volume never reached before.

But their prime position could be short-lived, however, if Cunard brings its *Queen Project* to fruition as a replacement for the *Queen Elizabeth II*. If the company orders the vessel envisaged, in a few years we will see the launch of a 150,000 ton liner, more than 386 meters (1260 feet) in length, for both cruises and the North Atlantic route. In one swoop, the *France* will lose the distinction of being the longest ship in the world (at 315 meters, 1033 feet), a record she has held since 1962.

Above: The atrium on the Vision of the Seas *clearly illustrates the analogy with American hotels.*
Left: from top to bottom: the Sovereign of the Seas, *the* Vision of the Seas *and the* Splendour of the Seas.

Far left: Although most
noted for the importance
of her outer appearance,
the Vision of the Seas
provides many attractions
in enclosed areas.
Left adjacent: a calm sea
for the Majesty of the Seas.
This liner is the last
in the "Of the seas" series.

The birth of a liner

The use of CAD (computer assisted design) predominates in defining the liner's details. This is a far cry from the draughtsmen's offices at the beginning of the century, in which the giants of the seas were mapped out.

Naval engineering is showing tremendous dynamism despite the closure of several prestigious shipyards, such as Vulkan at Bremen, and those of John Brown at the mouth of the Clyde near Glasgow.

Compared with the great age of the passenger ships, building a liner still conforms to the same basic plan. However, there is a growing use of simulation techniques, as well as a tendency to build the whole ship in a dry dock.

The main shipping companies

Today the cruise market is dominated by a small number of groups, of which the principal ones are, in order of importance:

The Carnival Cruise Line, which operates under its own flag and comprises, among others, Cunard, Holland America, Costa Crociere, Wind Star Sail Cruise, Croisieres Paquet and Seabourn Cruise;

The Norwegian group Royal Caribbean Cruise Line, which includes, in particular, the Greek company Celebrity Cruise, formerly Chandris;

The British group P & O (Penninsular & Oriental), which operates three large liners, which sometimes fly the flag of Princess Cruise, one of its nine subsidiaries;

The Norwegian Cruise Line, formerly known as Kloster Cruise, with its flagship the *Norway*, formerly the *France*.

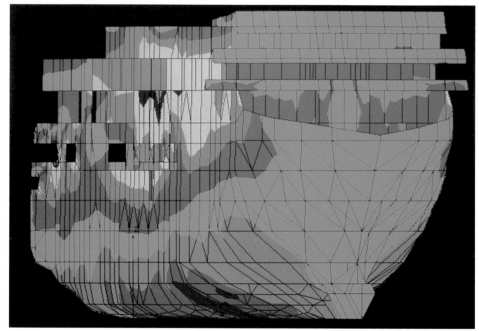

The basin of the lower parts of the hull enables the best aerodynamic water lines to be studied. These inspections take place before the profile of the hull is defined and are originally based on mockups. (Here, the NGV, Navire a Grande Vitesse "highspeed boat"

In 1995, the Jos.
L. Meyer shipyards
(Germany) delivered
two new ocean liners:
Century for
the Celebrity Cruises
company, in the
United States (top).
248 meters long,
and weighing
70,606 tons, it has
a 1,778-passenger
capacity. P & O
purchased the new
Oriana, designed for
1,975 passengers
(bottom). It can reach
a speed of 24 knots.

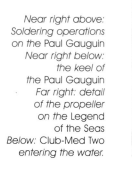

Near right above:
Soldering operations
on the Paul Gauguin
Near right below:
the keel of
the Paul Gauguin
Far right: detail
of the propeller
on the Legend
of the Seas
Below: Club-Med Two
entering the water.

The finishing work for the Sun Princess (top) for the P & O. Star Cruise purchased the Superstar Leo from the Meter shipyards (Germany). 268 meters longs, it can carry 2,800 passengers and reach a speed of 24 knots.

CROSS SECTION OF THE TITA

1 Crew's quarters   **2** Cargo hold   **3** Third-class cabins   **4** Mail room   **5** Promenade deck

6 Officers' quarters   **7** First-class cabins   **8** Swimming pool   **9** First-class dining room   **10** Second-class dining room

Glossary

ANCHOR
An implement for retaining a ship by dropping it to the sea's bottom

ANCHORAGE
A place for anchoring

BALLAST
A heavy material used to weigh down and steady a ship

BLUE RIBAND
A distinction awarded to the fastest ship on the North Atlantic route

BULWARK
The side of the ship projecting above the deck

CROW'S NEST
An elevated shelter for the lookout

DECKHOUSE
A room on deck

DISPLACEMENT
The quantity of water displaced by a ship afloat

DRAUGHT
The depth to which a ship sinks into the water

DRY DOCK
A dock that can be emptied of water

GANGWAY
A passage on a ship

HATCHWAY
An opening in the deck

HULL
The frame or body of a ship

KEEL
The part of a ship extending along the bottom from tem to stern and supporting the whole frame

LAUNCH
To cause a ship to slide into the water

LAY UP
To put into dock after dismantling

LIFEBOAT
A boat for saving shipwrecked people

LIST (VERB)
Heel over

MIXED CARGO
Passengers and freight

POOP
A high deck at the rear of a ship

PORTHOLE
A hole or opening in a ship's side for light and air

PORT (SIDE)

The left side of a ship

PROW

The foremost part of a ship

QUARTERS

Living accommodations.

REFIT

To fit out anew and repair

RUDDER

A flat structure hinged to the stern of the ship for steering

STARBOARD

The right side of a ship

STEERAGE

The part of a passenger ship offering the lowest fares

STERN

The rear of a ship

SUPERSTRUCTURE

A structure on the deck of a ship

TONNAGE

The carrying capacity of a ship in tons

TUG

A towing vessel

WINCH

A powerful type of hauling or lifting machine

Index

142

Bibliography

Great Passenger Ships of the World
Arnold Kludas
Patrick Stephens
PSL

Fifty Famous Liners
Frank O. Braynard et William Miller
Patrick Stephens
PSL

This book is dedicated to Denise Haussonn-Proust, passenger

The author wishes to thank especially
Claude Molteni de Villermont and Annie Madet (Musée de la Marine)

Key to illustrations for chapter headings
pp. 20-21 : *The Titanic.*
pp. 56-57 : The *Ile de France, France* and *Paris* in the port of Le Havre.
pp. 98-99 : The *France* leaves Le Havre for good, pulled by the tug *Abeille Provence.*
pp. 124-125 : *Majesty of the Seas.*

photographic credits

Roger-Viollet
p. 4 (right), p. 18, p. 24 (above), p. 30 (above), p. 31, p.46 (above), pp. 48-49, pp. 52-53, pp. 56-57, pp. 58-59, pp. 64-65, p. 66, p. 67 (below), pp. 70-71, p. 82, pp. 84-85, p. 86 (above), p. 87 (above, et en bas à droite), p. 90, p. 91 (en bas à gauche et en haut), p. 92, pp. 100-101, pp. 106-107.

Archives Claude Molteni de Villermont
p. 4 (left), p. 10 (en haut et en bas), p. 20, p. 30 (below), p. 34, pp. 50-51.

Gamma
p. 5, pp. 36-37, p. 38, p. 39 (below), p. 95 (above), p. 102 (above), pp. 114-115, pp. 120-121, pp. 124-125, pp. 126-127, pp. 128-129, pp. 130-131, pp. 132-133, pp. 134-135, pp. 136-137.

Musée de la Marine
p. 6, p. 7, p. 8, p. 9, p. 11, p. 12, p. 13, p. 14, p.15.

Photos de collections. DR
couverture, p. 7 (above), p. 17, p. 19, p. 20, pp. 22-23, pp. 24-25, pp. 26-27, pp. 28-29, p. 32 (above), p. 35, p. 39 (above), pp. 46-47, p. 53 (above), pp. 60-61, pp. 62-63, pp. 72-73, pp. 74-75, pp. 76-77, pp. 78-79, p. 80, p. 86 (below), pp. 88-89, pp. 94-95, pp. 96-97, pp. 102-103, p. 107 (above), pp. 108-109, pp. 110-111, p. 112-113, p. 116-117, pp. 118-119, pp. 122-123.

Explorer
p.16, pp. 32-33, pp. 40-41, pp. 42-43, pp. 44-45, pp. 54-55, p. 67 (above), pp. 68-69, p. 83, p. 87 (left), pp. 98-99, pp. 104-105, p. 126 (above), pp. 138-139.

Paul Telli :
p. 115 (above).

Devised and produced by **Copyright**
Graphics: Dorothée de Monfreid
Layout: Andréa Le Naour
Editorial co-ordination: Nicolas Jeanneau